THE EAP SOLUTION

CURRENT & FUTURE

Jerry Spice

THE EAP SOLUTION
CURRENT TRENDS & FUTURE ISSUES

Jerry Spicer, Editor

Hazelden®

First published January, 1987.

Copyright © 1987, Hazelden Foundation.
All rights reserved. No portion of this publication
may be reproduced in any manner without the written
permission of the publisher.

ISBN: 0-89486-405-X
Library of Congress Catalog Card Number 86-082533

Printed in the United States of America.

Editor's Note:
   Hazelden Educational Materials offers a variety of information on chemical dependency and related areas. Our publications do not necessarily represent Hazelden or its programs, nor do they officially speak for any Twelve Step organization.

To E.M.S.

CONTENTS

PREFACE AND ACKNOWLEDGMENTS

INTRODUCTION 1

CHAPTER ONE   EAP PROGRAM MODELS AND PHILOSOPHIES.........3

CHAPTER TWO   MANAGING EAP SERVICES.........................19

CHAPTER THREE   MARKETING 49

CHAPTER FOUR   RESEARCH.......................................77

CHAPTER FIVE   EVALUATION 99

CHAPTER SIX   CASE STUDIES 131

CHAPTER SEVEN   FUTURE ISSUES AND TRENDS 187

A FINAL NOTE 204

APPENDIXES 205

Figures and Tables

Figure 1	Dimensions of Employee Assistance Program Models	7
Figure 2	Decreased Productivity	11
Figure 3	Myths About Chemical Dependency Assessment	23
Figure 4	Hazelden EAP Quality Assurance Standards	48
Figure 5	Pricing Strategies	69
Figure 6	Components of EAP Research	80
Figure 7	Cost-Analysis Terms	88
Figure 8	Common Cost-Containment Strategies	90
Figure 9	Cost-Effectiveness Example	92
Figure 10	Measuring the Cost Impact of an EAP	93
Figure 11	Examples of Hazelden's Employee Assistance Services	136
Figure 12	EAP Caseload (Burlington Northern Railroad)	143
Figure 13	Chemical Dependency Cases (Burlington Northern Railroad)	144
Figure 14	Live for Life Referral Guidelines (Johnson and Johnson EAP)	152
Figure 15	Cumulative Utilization Rate (Johnson and Johnson EAP)	154
Figure 16	EAP Model — Current Contract	192
Figure 17	Model EAP Preferred Provider Services	193
Figure 18	Health Promotion Model	196
Figure 19	Assessment/Referral Form	208
Figure 20	Initial Client Questionnaire	209
Figure 21	One-Month Follow-Up Interview	210
Figure 22	Employee Assistance Program Survey	211
Figure 23	Customer Survey	215
Figure 24	Utilization Report	218
Figure 25	Sample Policy Statement	219
Table 1	Sample Calculation of Annual Utilization Rate	107
Table 2	Annual Program Utilization Rate	108
Table 3	Client Characteristics	109
Table 4	Employee Occupational Data	111
Table 5	Referral Sources	113
Table 6	Most Significant Assessed Problem	115
Table 7	Theoretical Comparison of Alcoholism Assessment	117

Table 8	Referrals to Community Resources	118
Table 9	One-Month Hazelden EAP Client Follow-Up	122
Table 10	Three-Month Follow-Up on Clients Assessed as Alcoholic	123
Table 11	Referral Recommendations by Hazelden EAP Counselors	124
Table 12	Comparison of Employee Job Performance Indicators	125
Table 13	Employee Referral Sources	127
Table 14	Most Significant Assessed Employee Problem	128
Table 15	Comparison of Employee and Dependent EAP Clients	129
Table 16	Job Performance Changes (Burlington Northern Railroad)	145
Table 17	Live for Life Assistance Program (Johnson and Johnson EAP)	149

Preface and Acknowledgments

Writing about the administration of employee assistance programs is an exciting opportunity. Few areas of health care have grown as rapidly in the last few years or hold as much promise of continued development. Not only are more employee assistance programs being implemented, there has also been a tremendous diversification in the field as new service models are developed that expand upon the original occupational alcoholism program.

The challenge of writing this book has been to encompass all of the current employee assistance program models and issues. Our purpose was to provide an overview of a complex field, without presuming to be the single source of information. Although Hazelden has a commitment to the external broadbrush model, the value and importance of developing alternatives in meeting the needs of a complex and diverse clientele is a theme throughout the book. (For a discussion of Hazelden's participation in the EAP field, see Chapter Seven.) To that end, we have sought authors who represent other models and new trends. Also, the authors were encouraged not to give as much attention to areas where information is available for further study. For example, we have not gone into detail on diagnosing and treating chemical dependency since so much good information exists on this topic. The section on research is not a primer, but a guide to using employee assistance program research in an applied, occupational setting. For further information, readers will find key references at the end of most chapters.

Our goal is not to pose as experts on "*the* Employee Assistance Program model," but to provide useful information on a broad field of human service. We have assumed that the administration of an EAP often requires the same skills and knowledge needed to successfully manage other health or human services. Therefore, we have not discussed the basics of management, such as planning or budgeting. Instead we have focused on unique attributes of employee assistance services or areas where special application by management is appropriate.

A last point concerns terminology. For the sake of interest and variation, many terms are used interchangeably (for example, chemical dependence, addiction, and substance abuse), and other terms, such as "company" are meant in the broadest sense, including management, employees, and union members.

I would like to acknowledge the assistance and contributions of my co-writers without whose assistance this would be a narrower and less usable work. All of us owe thanks to the many professionals and writers who have preceded us. Wherever possible we have acknowledged their contributions. However, we are solely responsible for our interpretation of their writings.

My special thanks to Judy Bontjes for her patience and perseverance in preparing the manuscript.

I hope this book will enable more employee assistance programs to be developed, and, as a result, more people will achieve healthy, high-quality lives.

Jerry Spicer
Center City
June, 1986

INTRODUCTION

EAPs — The Public Health Movement of the 1980s

The development of employee assistance programs has been similar to the growth of the public health field in general. We can understand what is happening in employee assistance programs by reviewing events in the public health movement.

To review these events, we can trace a simplified history that follows a series of discoveries and actions. First, scientists discovered that illnesses were caused by germs, bacteria, and other "invisible" agents. Second, once the causes were known, preventive measures and treatment were also discovered — sanitation, innoculation, pasteurization and all the "simple" precautions we take for granted today. As a result, life expectancy increased dramatically. But a third event that is sometimes overlooked had a tremendous impact on public health. This was the combined support for public health measures by private industry, government, and communities. There was initial opposition to the new theories on the etiology and treatment of illness, and members of the general public and the professional community were skeptical. However, as the evidence accumulated (the origins of epidemiology), public opinion shifted. American industry recognized the value of healthy, productive employees and the costs of poor public health, and gave its support to public health actions.

The development of employee assistance programs follows a similar course. We are emerging from a period of skepticism and distrust about treatment of chemical dependency and mental illness. Now we are recognizing that these "invisible" problems are resolvable, and there are direct, measurable benefits to the employer who has employees free of infectious and contagious diseases and from chemical dependency, mental health, and lifestyle diseases. These are exciting times for employee assistance programs. The social forces are with us. More people recognize the reality of mental illness, chemical dependency, and related problems, and accept

The EAP Solution

the humanistic and economic value of responding to these problems at the personal, community, political, and industrial levels. But we are not assured of success. The less effective programs must be improved, our results documented, and new models developed as we learn more about the workplace and the new problems employees will encounter in a changing world. I am excited about our opportunities, yet uneasy about how much we still have to learn about emotional and chemical dependency problems. This book is not written to give the "right" prescription, but to give you options to consider and alternatives to evaluate. The goal is to achieve health and wellness in the workplace through the teamwork of the employees, employer, and the employee assistance program professionals.

Overview of the Book

The diversity of employee assistance program models and services requires a broad perspective and an eye to the future. In the next chapter, I will briefly review the development of the employee assistance program field, discuss some typical current models, and briefly note some emerging models that will be explained in the last chapter. Chapter Two, written by Timothy Plant, focuses on the basic services of an employee assistance program: counseling, communications, and management consultation. The employee assistance program field is highly competitive; in Chapter Three, Gary Hestness and Vincent Hyman outline the basics of marketing from planning a product to closing the sale. Donald Jones and Patricia Owen focus on evaluation, cost-benefit analysis, and research in Chapters Four and Five. Chapter Six includes shorter monographs by several authors who provide their insights and experiences in working in a variety of settings from the union/labor model to proprietary models. Finally, we conclude with an analysis of where we might be going as emerging models and issues are presented.

1

EAP Program Models and Philosophies
Jerry Spicer, M.H.A.

Jerry Spicer is the Director of Hazelden's Employee Assistance Services and a member of Hazelden's senior management. In addition to the administration of employee assistance services, he is also responsible for consultation and training services. He has authored several articles and books on management and research and teaches in both Hazelden's continuing education workshops and the University of Minnesota's program in mental health administration. He has worked in the chemical dependency field for over twelve years, at Hazelden and in Canada, and has a master's degree in hospital and health services administration from the University of Minnesota. He is a certified member of the Association of Mental Health Administrators and the American College of Addiction Treatment Administrators.

The EAP Solution

Historical Developments and Current Approaches

The first employee assistance program was probably an informal service provided at no cost to employees by a fellow employee recovering from alcoholism. The growth of Alcoholics Anonymous during the 1940s impacted the workplace as more recovering people returned to their jobs carrying the message of A.A. They demonstrated to their employers the value and effectiveness of intervention. During the fifties and sixties, occupational alcoholism programs were implemented in hundreds of companies and unions, and support for the concept came from state and local governments and health care providers. As employers became more involved in employee assistance, the emphasis shifted to focus on deteriorating job performance as a means for identifying the employee requiring help. During this period external contractors became involved in consultation, training, and service delivery. Local associations and national professional associations such as the Association of Labor-Management Administrators and Consultants on Alcoholism (ALMACA) were developed to provide a forum for the new EAP practitioners to share ideas.

The next major stage was the development of the "broadbrush" model. As employees began to request help for problems in addition to alcohol and other drugs, EAP practitioners found it necessary to broaden the scope of their services. Emotional problems also affected job performance decline, and these problems could not be ignored if the EAP was a performance-based model. Finally, the proponents of the broadbrush model cited evidence that this model encouraged employees to safely present problems other than chemical dependency, and that the assessment process could find the underlying chemical dependency.

Currently, programs of all types offer EAP services — from single-person companies to large for-profit enterprises to the in-house counselor. The occupational alcoholism program is prevalent as is the broadbrush approach. Occupational mental health, health promotion, and cost-control services are becoming increasingly common as employers seek to cope with changing times.

EAP Program Models and Philosophies

This flexibility in functioning and purpose is a two-edged sword. EAPs have historically been able to adapt to new issues and needs, and are what the employer and employees require. However, the EAP field may be in danger of increased fragmentation and internal conflict as all these divergent opinions are voiced. (We should not assume that this is only an EAP issue. The health care and the employee benefits fields are undergoing rapid changes that make future predictions uncertain.) Although the future is not predictable, there are commonalities in service and operation that characterize employee assistance programs and distinguish them from other employer or health care services.

Current and Emerging Models

An employee assistance program can be defined as an employer- or labor-sponsored service designed to assist employees, and often their dependents, in finding help for drug, mental/emotional, family, health, or other personal problems. EAPs are typically funded and supported by an employer or union, and are considered an employee benefit as well as a means of improving employee (and therefore employer) productivity through reducing personal problems that may negatively affect an employee's job performance.

Beyond the focus on employees and the workplace, there is a tremendous variation among EAPs. The focus of the EAP may be alcohol or other drugs, personal problems in general (the broadbrush model), health promotion, or some combination of these. Historically, employee assistance programs were designed to address the problems of alcoholism in the workplace. In the last few years, new EAPs have been designed to deal with a broad range of emotional/mental problems and most recently with wellness or health promotion. New arrivals on the EAP scene include the EAP marketing and cost-containment models. In the marketing model, the EAP service is discounted or provided free as a way of increasing referrals to the provider. As a current example, a preferred provider organization on the West Coast now gives a company's employees free EAP (and low-cost health screening services) as part of a preferred provider package. A very new, but a strong trend for the future, is to utilize the EAP as a gatekeeper or controller for health care costs. In this model, the EAP provider (whether internal or external) will be expected to address issues of cost-effectiveness and cost-benefit.

An EAP can be located within the company as part of a personnel/human resources, medical, or other department. These internal or in-house programs are in contrast to external models where services are delivered, usually under contract by an external organization such as an EAP vendor, hospital, or mental health center. There is also a current trend where employers may use a combination of internal and external services. External vendors are likely to be used to deliver new services or regular services to dispersed employees.

The services provided by an EAP can include information and referral, short-term counseling, client follow-up, training, education and communication materials, management consultation, statistical reporting, health screening, and so on (see Figure 1).

In short, there exists no predominant EAP model. EAPs vary according to the needs of the employer and employee, and new models are emerging as this book is published (see Chapter Six). What EAPs have in common is the shared concept that personal problems affect the workplace, and the EAP is an effective way to address these problems, thereby benefiting the employees' general emotional and physical health and the company's bottom line.

Commonalities in the EAP Field

Employee assistance programs typically are similar in philosophy and operation.

1. *Company Support:* Employee assistance programs are a benefit provided by the company's management or labor, or both. The company perceives the EAP to be a benefit reflecting a modern, employee-oriented management philosophy and a service that will have an economic benefit by improving the productivity and health of its employees. The company's support is evidenced in the funding of the EAP where the service is free to employees and paid for

EAP Program Models and Philosophies

Figure 1
Dimensions Of Employee Assistance Program Models

Relative Age: Older → Newer → Emerging

Program Focus	Program Location Internal	Program Location External
Alcohol or other drug focused	X	
Broadbrush/comprehensive	X	X
Health promotion/wellness	X	X
Marketing strategy		X
Cost-containment agent	X	X

X = typical services

Program Services

Traditional Services → Newer Services

- Assessment, referral
- Short-term counseling
- Aftercare/follow-up
- Management consultation
- Education, training & communication; policy development
- Research & statistical reporting
- Utilization review, admission certification
- Case management
- Benefits consultation
- Health promotion
- *Crisis Intervention*

The EAP Solution

by the company, whether an internal or external model is used.

2. *Intervention in the Workplace:* A unique aspect of EAPs, compared to other forms of health care, is the focus on the workplace. Services are often delivered on-site, and job performance decline is used as a signal for referral. The provider also recognizes early intervention and referral as effective when the client is still employed and when the employer is committed to helping retain a valued employee.

3. *The EAP Partnership:* To achieve excellence, the EAP requires support and involvement from all levels of management, labor, and the practitioner. This support is demonstrated through funding, training, policy development, service delivery, and ongoing management. All partners must not only want an EAP but they must use it.

4. *Confidentiality and Accessibility:* Hazelden's research has consistently found that confidentiality and accessibility are critical aspects of an EAP. Employees and management want accessible services and clear policies and procedures that protect confidentiality. The stigma and denial associated with chemical dependency and mental health problems require special attention to assure that people are receiving professional care.

5. *Short-Term Services:* The EAP practitioner or counselor enhances, but does not replace or duplicate the services available under the employee's health plan. Assessment, referral, aftercare, follow-up, and perhaps short-term counseling are the usual activities of the EAP professional. The EAP practitioner helps employees recognize their problems, find help, and then monitors these services and assists in returning the employee to the workplace. To a great extent, the EAP staff are case managers and are most directly involved before and after treatment.

6. *Management/Labor Orientation:* Perhaps the most unique aspect of an EAP is its close link to a company's management and labor. Whether internal or external, alcohol- or mental health-focused,

EAP Program Models and Philosophies

management- or union-sponsored, the EAP bridges the gap between the provider, the employee, and a company's management. The EAP professional is more than a counselor; he is also a trainer, a management and benefits consultant, and at times an organizational psychologist. Because each company and work force have unique needs, no EAP operates the same in all settings. Flexibility and a strong repertoire of skills are requirements for EAP staff members. The EAP is required to interrelate with a variety of management functions including the company's benefits, medical, and personnel departments.

The EAP and Productivity

The company's (by using the word *company* we include management, unions, and employees) interest in having an EAP is predicated on two advantages. First of all, by having the EAP, the supervisor is not expected to be a counselor or clinician. If a supervisor believes he or she has an employee with a personal problem, the supervisor can recommend the EAP to that employee, or if the employee's job performance is suffering from what may be a personal problem, the supervisor can make a formal referral to an EAP. Secondly, we have come to recognize that personal problems do affect job performance and that employers can and should provide ways for employees to get help — not only as a humane management practice but also to have healthy, productive employees.

But the issue of employee productivity is a complex problem, and we must be careful not to oversell the impact an EAP can have on the bottom line. A brief listing of the elements that contribute to a worker's productivity might be as follows:

1. *Technology and Tools*: To be productive an employee needs to have the right equipment.
2. *Training and Education*: Not only are the right tools needed, but the employee also needs to know how to use them.
3. *Management and Supervision:* The efforts and activities of employees must be coordinated and planned.

The EAP Solution

4. *Employee Attitudes and Morale:* Employees who take pride in their work and their company will contribute to the success of the firm.
5. *Employee Emotional and Physical Health:* To be productive, an employee needs the psychological and physical resources to accomplish the job.

Obviously an EAP cannot address all of these areas of productivity. The typical EAP focuses primarily on the emotional and physical health of the individual employee. By directly improving the employee's health, the EAP provider assumes (and indeed the data supports the assumption) the employee's productivity will improve as absenteeism, accidents, and lowered concentration improve (see Figure 2).

The EAP can have a secondary impact on productivity by improving supervisory skills in spotting and documenting job performance declines through the training typically provided to supervisors. Finally, the EAP can improve overall morale. Employees affect other employees, and when troubled employees improve so does the work group. And in a general sense the EAP is seen as a worthwhile employee benefit and gives employees a favorable image of their employer.

Given the complexity of productivity, the EAP can be only one part of a general plan to make employees and the company more productive. As discussed in later chapters, there is clear evidence that the troubled employees do have job performance declines associated with their problems, and as the problems improve, so does job performance. But productivity for the entire company is a much more complex issue and often depends on forces outside the control of the EAP.

In conclusion, employee assistance programs have experienced a rapid growth and development, and will continue to evolve in response to changes in business, health care, and employees. In the next chapters various authors will review some specific EAP functions, and in the concluding chapter we will return to the issue of future trends.

EAP Program Models and Philosophies

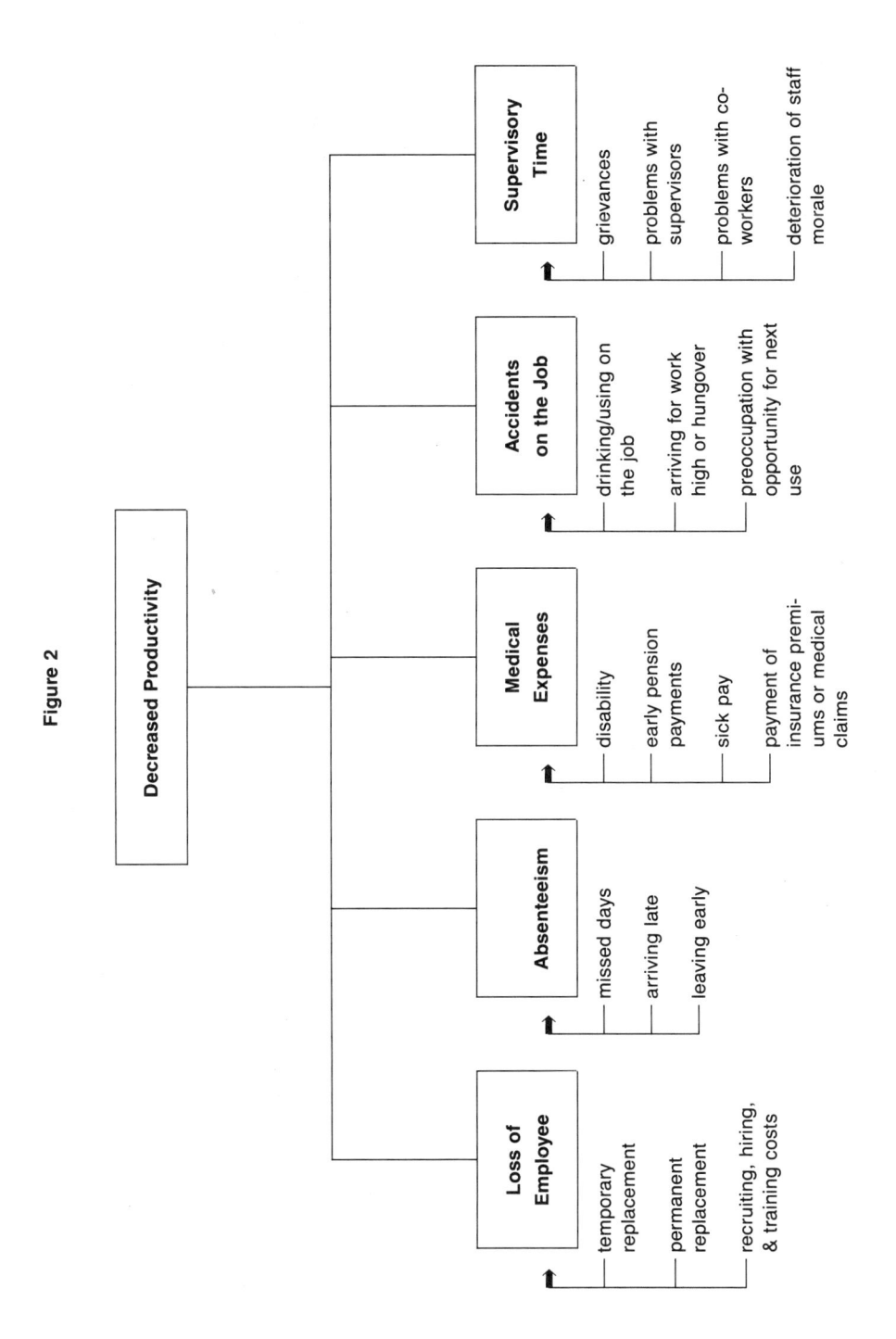

Figure 2

Decreased Productivity

- **Loss of Employee**
  - temporary replacement
  - permanent replacement
  - recruiting, hiring, & training costs

- **Absenteeism**
  - missed days
  - arriving late
  - leaving early

- **Medical Expenses**
  - disability
  - early pension payments
  - sick pay
  - payment of insurance premiums or medical claims

- **Accidents on the Job**
  - drinking/using on the job
  - arriving for work high or hungover
  - preoccupation with opportunity for next use

- **Supervisory Time**
  - grievances
  - problems with supervisors
  - problems with co-workers
  - deterioration of staff morale

Internal and External Models
Brenda Blair, M.B.A.

Brenda R. Blair is President of Blair Associates, a management consulting firm which provides employee assistance program consultation and training services. She has over ten years of experience with EAPs in a variety of settings, including large corporations, federal and state governments, and hospitals. She has authored books and articles on EAPs and alcoholism in the workplace. Her M.B.A. is from Northwestern University.

Employee assistance programs are commonly provided according to either the internal program model or the external contractor model. Other mechanisms include creative structuring such as consortium approaches or a combination of internal and external programs. Since most employers will find either the internal program model, external contractor model, or an internal/external combination model sufficient to their needs, those approaches will be discussed here.

Definition of Models

In the internal model, employee assistance program services are provided solely by an employee or employees of the company. Smaller organizations may employ a single EAP professional, either full- or part-time, while larger organizations may have several staff who share the various administrative, consultative, and assessment and referral functions. Internal programs are most commonly structured as part of an employer's medical department, human resources department, or as a completely separate department.

In the external contractor model, EAP services are offered by employees of an external organization whose work is secured on a contractual basis. Staffing patterns may include full-time or part-time staff who work at the employer's facilities, at the offices of the external contractor, or a combination of locations. External contractors may offer a full or partial range of EAP services; some provide only program development and initial

EAP Program Models and Philosophies

training, some concentrate only on the assessment and referral function, while others may include ongoing employee education projects and other continuing activities. External EAP contractors may be employed by independent private firms which specialize in EAPs, by hospitals and health care organizations, by chemical dependence treatment organizations, by community mental health centers, by family service centers, and by a variety of other organizations that have entered the EAP field in recent years.

Advantages and Disadvantages of Program Models

A major benefit of internal programs is the ability of the internal EAP professional to become familiar with the formal and informal management and political systems within the employing organization, thus permitting the EAP to function more effectively within these systems. Internal EAP staff are frequently more aware of the work-related pressures affecting managers and employees and, as a result, can often intervene in problem situations before a crisis occurs. Also, internal EAP professionals may inspire greater employee confidence in the program, since "the EAP person is here and understands the kinds of problems we have."

Another advantage stems from the internal professional's capability to work continually within the system to assess, modify, and improve the program. While an internal professional can arrange changes by using the services of various internal company departments, similar changes in an external program may require contract modification.

As with the advantages, the major disadvantages derive from the fact that the EAP is part of the system. Employees of the organization may not view the EAP as a sufficiently confidential, safe haven from the political fluctuations of their daily work life. Because the EAP staff work directly for the same employing organization that their potential clients do, some employees will feel uncomfortable using an internal program and may prefer to consult someone external to the organization who may be perceived as more confidential in their approach. In both the internal and external model, the perception of confidentiality will depend greatly on the climate of trust within the organization and the abilities of the specific EAP professionals who provide service to adhere to the highest standards of confidentiality.

An advantage associated with the external contractor model is the convenience it can provide to a small- or medium-sized employer who does not have the need or resources for internal EAP staff. Hiring an external EAP firm to provide services allows the employer to acquire EAP expertise without being concerned about supervising the EAP staff, providing costly personnel benefits, assuring that the staff receive ongoing professional training, and similar issues which are the responsibility of the contractor. Of course, it is important that the external contractor perform these staffing functions well. For example, if the external contractor's own human resources management practices cause low morale or frequent turnover among the EAP professionals, the effectiveness of the EAP would be diminished.

Another advantage of the external contractor model is that the external contractor may feel more responsibility to provide program evaluation and quality control mechanisms than an internal employee. While much of the pioneering work in program evaluation design was conducted by internal EAPs, external contractors have been the leaders in recent years. Since external contractors are providing services for a number of clients, they have a larger data base with which to compare programs and to monitor differences in program effectiveness. With increased competition among external contractors, there have been incentives for external contractors to accurately evaluate their programs in order to secure and renew contracts with employers. Of course, high-quality EAP professionals will be concerned about monitoring and program evaluation questions regardless of whether or not they are internal employees or work for an external contractor.

A major disadvantage of the external contractor model can occur if the contractor uses a single approach for serving all its accounts and pays insufficient attention to the needs of each employer organization. For example, an external contractor may not take the

EAP Program Models and Philosophies

time to learn enough about the employer's benefits package, organizational constraints, disciplinary process, concerns of management, style of management-employee interactions, and similar workplace issues. If the external contractor is seeking economies of scale at the expense of individual employers, the quality of EAP programming will suffer.

Costs

In any given situation, one or the other program model will be less expensive, depending, among other things, on the size and location of the employee population and the competitive climate for EAP contractors in a particular location. With an internal program, the employer assumes all EAP expenses, such as staff salary and benefits, employee promotional materials, supervisory training films, secretarial support for the EAP staff, staff travel and training expenses, office supplies and overhead, and so on.

With an external contractor model, a single contractual agreement covers all expenses, with the external contractor assuming responsibility for paying appropriate salaries and benefits and for assuring that sufficient operating funds are allocated to the EAP.

In either case, the cost of the EAP may increase. In an internal program, salaries and general operating expenses normally increase slightly each year; with the external contractor model, the fee may need to be renegotiated with each contract renewal. Some organizations will prefer an internal program because budgetary authority affords greater control of the program; others will prefer the convenience of a single contractual agreement with an external contractor.

Choosing a Model

In deciding which model to implement, an employer should consider the demographics of the employee work force, the organizational factors which would aid or hinder the work of the EAP, the perceptions of the employees regarding confidentiality, the corporate culture's attitude toward "insiders" vs. "outsiders," the comparative costs of either model, and the degree of control over the EAP desired by the employer. Creative

The EAP Solution

program designs are becoming more common. For example, a company may choose to provide internal staff in locations with large numbers of employees and use external contracts in locations with fewer employees. Adding customized requirements to the contracts of external contractors is another option. Careful planning and selection of program models can result in an employee assistance program which truly meets a company's needs.

References

Blair, B., "Selecting an EAP contractor that will meet company needs," *Occupational Health and Safety*, Nov/Dec, 1984.

Blair, B., *Hospital Employee Assistance Programs*, Chicago, IL, American Hospital Publishing, 1985.

Brenton, M., *Help for the Troubled Employee*, New York, NY, Public Affairs Pamphlets, 1982.

Kurtz, N. R., B. Googins, and Howard W. Googins, *Occupational Alcoholism: An Annotated Bibliography*, Toronto, Canada, Addiction Research Foundation, 1984.

Wrich, J. T., *The Employee Assistance Program: Updated for the 1980's*, Center City, MN, Hazelden Educational Materials, 1980. Order no. 1015.

2

MANAGING EAP SERVICES
Timothy Plant, M.A.

Tim Plant, formerly the manager of Hazelden's Employee Assistance Services, currently manages Hazelden's southwest regional programs. He has worked in the EAP field for over ten years and has a master's degree in social service administration from the University of Chicago.

Whatever the topic or current issue (cost efficiency, standards and licensing, HMOs), effective delivery of employee assistance program services remains the central objective and challenge for EAP practitioners. Although "specialists" (counselors, salespeople, trainers) play a vital role, particularly in large EAP departments, a broadly trained EAP practitioner has the necessary skills to meet the needs of employees and complex business organizations. Whether advocating for clients with community resources or cutting through bureaucratic red tape within an organization, this ability matches well with the client's need for prompt, effective help in directly resolving problems.

Counseling

Is EAP counseling simply good counseling, regardless of setting? Is it any different from counseling done in another setting, whether hospital, family service, chemical dependency treatment center, or private mental health clinic? While the counseling skills required may be similar, their application can be very different. The EAP counselor must have a full and practical understanding of the world of work — the importance of work in the client's life, the complexities of the business world, and labor-management relationships. This knowledge is essential to the process of problem evaluation, assessing appropriate referral options, and negotiating return to work following treatment. EAP counselors must have the skills and formal training to competently assess both chemical dependency and the variety of problems presented by diverse employee and family populations.

Although EAPs are primarily concerned with identification of chemical dependency, they must also address the inappropriate drug use — short of addiction — which is a pervasive occupational problem. Inappropriate drug use represents potential or early stage dependency as well as serious social and health costs associated with problem use.

Finally, EAP counselors should function first as advocates for their client's needs while also representing the interests of the sponsoring employer. Referrals provided must consider the best interests of the client, given the limitations of insurance coverage and available resources. Wherever possible, particularly when the EAP provider is also part of a treatment center, the client must be given choices between the best quality and least costly service options.

Assessment

Assessment is a process leading to mutual identification of the nature and extent of problems of an individual or significant others. Identification of problems is a major service provided to employee assistance clients. The first step involves building a relationship by using good empathic skills to demonstrate acceptance, listening, and understanding of the client. EAP counselors are trained to evaluate the nature of the concerns presented by the client and to develop and discuss recommendations for action with the client. Educational methods, such as pamphlets or tapes, are used to help clients personally evaluate their problem.

The objectives of assessment counseling are
- to identify and evaluate the client's problems
- to seek immediate problem resolution when possible
- to reach agreement with the client on those problems that require further assistance

Employees or family members who voluntarily contact the EAP receive direct, confidential help. The employee's supervisor is not informed unless the employee requests notification and signs a written release of information.

Five basic steps are followed in conducting an assessment process in an employee assistance program setting:
1. *Familiarizing* — establishing a relationship
2. *Interviewing* — gathering extensive historical data
3. *Educating/Confronting* — providing information and support for problem recognition
4. *Motivating/Referring* — disposition of the case
5. *Follow-up* — continued clinical case management and support.

Assessing Chemical Dependency Problems

Assessment is rarely a single event. Most often it is a process occurring over time, beginning long before a client walks into the EAP counselor's office and continuing through the recommended treatment. Clients with alcohol or other drug problems have considered the nature of their problem themselves and have been confronted by others. The professional has a vital role in guiding the assessment process toward a healthy conclusion.

Identification of alcohol and other drug problems must be mutually accepted by both the professional helper and the client. Chemical dependency, except at its latest stages, is not easily diagnosed by any "litmus test" or simple physical measure. Therefore the client needs to be involved in the process from the beginning and must take responsibility for the final decision on chemical dependency. The counselor must be trained to avoid the common myths about chemical dependency assessment (see Figure 3).

When assessing chemical dependency, it is also important to consider assessment of other problems such as inappropriate drug use, mental health problems, sexual abuse, and other family problems. The assessment interview furnishes the best, and perhaps only, opportunity to discover these issues. It is also common to find health problems related to chemical dependency. There are occasions when a client's chemical misuse simply masks the dependency of a significant other person or the existence of a serious health problem, e.g., an eating disorder. In any case, the professional counselor has an opportunity to identify where a client really needs help. The goal of the assessment is determining the existence of chemical dependency, while identifying related inappropriate drug use problems as well as other significant health or emotional problems. The next step for the counselor is to help the client act on this shared information by achieving a linkage or referral to the next appropriate level of care, whether that be treatment, an educational program, or a self-help group.

Information

Potential clients will call the EAP for information about the program and how to use it. A function of the counselor, as well as support staff, is to provide information that will enhance the possibility that the clients will use the program when they need it. Callers are offered information about available services and are provided telephone counseling when appropriate. An in-person appointment at an accessible location should be offered as soon as possible.

Crises Intervention

Twenty-four hour access, where it can be offered, makes it possible for the employee or family member to use services during crises. A significant number of

Managing EAP Services

Figure 3
Myths About Chemical Dependency Assessment

Myth	Reality
The client has to "hit bottom" or be in a very severe crisis before it's worth trying to help.	Clients may be motivated to accept earlier intervention with significant other support.
Client must be verbally abused in a punitive confrontation to be motivated to accept help.	Constructive confrontation can be positive and supportive.
Alcohol or other drug misuse is a symptom of an underlying problem.	Once the disease of chemical dependency exists, any initial cause may be irrelevant to the primary treatment.
Treat the presented problem (marital, depression, etc.) and wait to see if the chemical use problem improves.	If chemical dependency is the real problem, functioning will continue to deteriorate in all life areas.
I, the professional, should be able to provide all of the help myself.	Specialized help may be in the client's best interest and will free the therapist to play an ongoing supportive role.
I can't help and must refer out immediately.	Use trust already established to maintain as much continuity in relationships as possible, while seeking outside help.
Counselors require only personal experience with chemical dependency to be effective.	Motivation and skills come with personal experience, yet formal training in the EAP field and appropriate credentialling is necessary.
I only need to be concerned with screening for chemical dependency.	Assessment affords a chance to identify earlier patterns of chemical misuse and to provide educational intervention.
Everyone who misuses alcohol or other drugs is dependent.	Each case requires an individualized assessment.
All clients need _____ (the treatment I received, to try AA first, etc.).	Each case requires an individualized treatment plan.

evening and weekend callers appear to be people affected by alcohol and other drug problems. The after-hours counselor can offer support and guidance for immediate, specific problems, as well as referrals to emergency medical and counseling services. In-person follow-up sessions provide the opportunity for thorough problem exploration, including input from significant others and referral for needed care.

Referral Services

After identifying a client's problems, the counselor refers the client to the most suitable community resource. When making a referral, the EAP counselor should

- consider the client's location, ability to pay, cultural background, and other special needs
- when possible, identify two or three possible community resources
- help the employee contain health care costs by identifying free or cost-effective resources
- explain that the client is responsible for the cost of any services not covered by the employee's health insurance
- explain which services are covered by the employee's health insurance

In selecting a helping resource for alcoholic or mentally ill clients, a counselor may consider Twelve Step programs such as Alcoholics Anonymous or Emotions Anonymous, a nonresidential evening hour treatment program, or long-term residential treatment. The counselor's decision would be based on an assessment of the severity of the problem, the employer's health insurance coverage and sick leave policies, the client's support system of family and friends, and the relative cost of each option.

Clients with complex problems cannot be expected to make complicated decisions about all possible options. The counselor should help put the client's problems in perspective and set up the plan of action that is most likely to succeed.

Managing EAP Services

Follow-Up

Once the client has been referred to a community resource, the counselor monitors the client's progress through telephone and in-person follow-up. The purpose of client follow-up is to ensure a successful referral and to keep the employer informed of the client's progress (when appropriate and consistent with federal confidentiality guidelines). Regular contact with the client and community resource provides confirmation of the client's participation, gives feedback on the nature of the client's progress, and helps the counselor develop additional treatment recommendations. The cooperative relationship between the counselor and the community resource results in efficient and effective help for each client.

Specific follow-up standards depend on the type of problems identified, the client's reason for seeing the counselor, and the employer's specifications. For example, a self-referred client might require only brief follow-up over a few weeks, while an employer-referred client should be in contact with a counselor on a regular basis over several months or up to a year following return to a productive work pattern. Chemical dependency cases, as well as serious mental health and life-threatening situations, must be followed up over an extended period by the counselor in order to assure that the client has achieved stable recovery.

Short-Term Counseling

A trend in EAPs is for the program to provide short-term (from eight to ten sessions per problem incident) counseling as a cost-effective alternative to external referral. Many problems presented to EAP staff are, in fact, amenable to planned, short-term task-oriented or problem-solving counseling. Typical problems, such as marital or significant relationship conflict, reactive depression, job or career stress/conflict, or adjustment to a sobriety program, can be addressed through specific short-term treatment plans which involve the client, or family, or both, in shaping behavior change to alleviate target problems.

The EAP Solution

Areas which cannot be effectively addressed through short-term counseling alone, such as primary chemical dependency treatment, sexual abuse or incest therapy, or treatment for serious psychiatric disturbances, can continue to be addressed through timely referral to outside organizations and subsequent follow-up by the EAP staff.

Referral Consultation

EAP counselors must be available to consult with supervisors, managers, and other formal referents (labor, medical, human resources) on the process of referring their employees to the program. Just as clients who finally decide to get help want to act "now," so do their supervisors. Access to EAP services greatly enhances the prospect that management will obtain a major objective of the program — to effectively intervene with problems that impair job performance.

The EAP counselor provides information, advice on approaching the employee, and a source of support for the manager in taking action even when it is difficult. The referent and counselor review the documentation of any job performance problem and disciplinary action history, discuss how to make a referral to the EAP, and determine future mutual role expectations. The counselor is also able to direct the manager to other helpful sources, including the organization's human resource, employee relations, benefits, and labor representatives, where appropriate. Following referral, the counselor is available to the supervisor for follow-up support and, where the employee has signed a release of information, mutual feedback about employee progress. When formal treatment is conducted, the counselor arranges a discharge planning conference with the supervisor and employee to review the employee's progress in treatment and to discuss plans to return to work.

Training

The goal of employee assistance program training is to facilitate program understanding and thereby promote effective use of the EAP.

Managing EAP Services

Executive Briefings

In an executive briefing, EAP trainers provide brief executive orientation sessions at the work site. Trainers explain the EAP and summarize the supervisory training and employee orientations, emphasizing the benefits of EAP to the organization. These sessions help gain the top management support necessary for a successful EAP.

Supervisory Training

Supervisory/management trainings are presented in a three- to four-hour session to groups of twenty to twenty-five.

Sessions are designed to accomplish three objectives:
- to teach supervisors the purpose of employee assistance
- to teach supervisors how to use the EAP
- to build confidence in the program's function as a performance management tool

Training focuses on building support for the EAP and on skill development, especially documenting job performance problems and referring employees to the EAP counselor. Lectures, case histories, discussions, and practice sessions prepare supervisors to use the program.

Basic content covers four areas:
- types of employee problems and their effect on co-workers, supervisors, and job performance
- how employee assistance helps employees in trouble
- how employee assistance benefits the supervisor
- job performance documentation, referring an employee to the program, and consultation with the counselor

Employee Orientation

Employee orientation sessions last about one hour and are designed to accomplish three objectives:
- to build trust in the program and the counselor
- to teach employees how to use the EAP
- to encourage self-referrals

The EAP Solution

Employees learn that the EAP is free and confidential. Topics include the scope of problems that affect employees and their families: marital, family, relationships, alcohol and other drugs, emotional, psychological, legal, financial, and health. Employees learn how they or a family member can directly contact their counselor and what to expect at an assessment and referral counseling session.

Education/Prevention Session

As a follow-up to employee orientations, it is helpful to provide specific educational sessions about topics of interest to employees such as "Making Stress Work for You," "Family Relationships," "Managing Money," "Eating Right — Good Nutrition." These sessions, lasting about one hour, can be provided over the lunch hour or after work, and may involve the family.

These educational sessions not only serve as a way to remind everyone that the EAP is available to help solve problems, but they also broaden the impact of EAPs by providing a direct educational service to the many employees who attend but will not become clients.

Program Communications and Promotion

Even with the best EAP counseling services available, if no one knows about it or trusts the service, it cannot provide the necessary help. It is important to develop and implement a publicity plan for program implementation and ongoing promotion.

Some of the most effective types of program communications include 1) wallet cards, 2) brochures highlighting EAP services and specific problem areas addressed, 3) specific publications developed to aid supervisors in fulfilling their EAP referral responsibilities, and 4) articles in company newsletters. Wallet cards for employees and family members include contact information (phone numbers, office addresses) along with information about problems addressed. (See the Appendix for examples).

Perhaps the single most effective promotional item is a brochure highlighting a problem area addressed by the program, such as "Problems in the Family," "Alcohol and Other Drug Problems," "Stress," or "Questions

Managing EAP Services

and Answers About Your EAP". Hazelden has developed over twenty such topical brochures to be mailed directly to employees and families at home, or distributed at the work site. In Hazelden's experience, it is more effective to send the brochures directly to the employee's home. This ensures the word about EAP services will get out directly to eligible family members so they know they can directly contact the EAP. Hazelden has documented a 50 percent increase in program utilization during the month following a mailing to employee households.

Supervisory booklets such as "Job Performance Review" and "Problems on the Job (A Supervisor's Guide to Coping)" (both available through Hazelden Educational Materials, Box 176, Pleasant Valley Road, Center City, MN 55012, order nos. 1369 and 1403) are useful both as supplementary training aids as well as reference material for the busy supervisor. Although the key information is contained in such a reference, it is recognized and reinforced during training that this material is not a substitute for communication and guidance from EAP staff on completing a specific referral.

Program Implementation and Management

Successful program implementation requires a carefully developed and managed plan. During the implementation stage the EAP provider should continuously assess the company's needs and develop solutions to meet them. The following steps are suggested, based on the experience of Hazelden Employee Assistance Services.

1. *Implementation Date* — Set a target date for the initial availability of counseling services to employees and family. Do not attempt to provide counseling services until all steps have been completed.
2. *Policy/Procedures Development* — Develop specific guidelines and policies for the EAP. Included are areas such as confidentiality, disciplinary policies, and overall program philosophy. Get management and union approval. (See the Appendix for a sample policy statement used by Hazelden Employee Assistance Services.)

The EAP Solution

3. *Selection and Training of Program Coordinator* — An individual should be designated by the organization as the EAP Coordinator. This person is responsible for overall coordination of program activity for the company, including scheduling of training and other program publicity, evaluation of program activity reports, and troubleshooting to insure the quick resolution of any problems and ongoing program support.

4. *Obtain Union Advocacy and Support for the EAP* — It is critical for program survival and effectiveness that the EAP staff and company management obtain union support for the implementation of the EAP. The methods for accomplishing this will vary with the setting, but may include meetings with key union representatives to obtain union input into significant program implementation decisions (such as office location or staffing), participation of union representatives in an EAP Advisory Committee or Committee of Concern, union attendance at EAP training sessions, review of significant policy/procedural components to insure union support, and, where necessary, sharing endorsements from other unions who have had favorable experience with an EAP.

5. *Program Publicity* — Development and processing of printed materials such as wallet cards, supervisory and employee brochures, and posters, should be completed well in advance of projected distribution dates.

6. *Review and Summarize Health Insurance Coverage* — All applicable health insurance policies should be reviewed to determine coverage for mental health and chemical dependency treatment. This information can be summarized in a useful format for quick reference by EAP counseling staff prior to delivery of counseling services. If coverage appears to be inadequate or unclear for specific problems, the EAP provider should request further explanation and work with the company to resolve potential problems. The EAP counselor should be prepared to advise the employee seeking treatment of expected insurance coverage and any personal expenses related to treatment.

Managing EAP Services

7. *Scheduling of EAP Training* — The dates should be identified for presentations to top management (Executive Briefings), Management Training, Employee Orientations or other trainings. Give the EAP Coordinator a dry run of the training, and allow time for changes in the content of materials.

8. *Administrative Planning* — Other information will be needed by the EAP staff to deliver services. (For example, the company's organizational structure.) It is important that the EAP staff have a good working knowledge of the nature of the employer's business and typical job-related problems. New referral resource may be necessary for a new contract.

9. *Ongoing Program Management* — A plan should be established for periodic review of the EAP which involves program staff, clients, and key individuals in the organization. Whether EAP services are provided by in-house employees or on an external contractual basis, the program must be dynamic and flexible enough to meet the changing needs of the work environment while maintaining strong continuity of service quality. The well-managed EAP will successfully serve five to ten percent of the employees each year. The EAP should have a plan that includes annual objectives and strategies to meet the changing needs of the employer and the employees.

Supervising Clinical Staff
Mary Ellen Lukina-Wiersma, M.S.W.

Mary Ellen Lukina-Wiersma supervises over a dozen staff people responsible for direct services to clients as well as contract management duties. She has several years of experience in the EAP field and has worked at Hazelden for four years. She has a M.S.W. from the University of Minnesota.

Supervising employee assistance program counselors is a relatively new challenge. Most employee assistance programs have been small with limited staff, yet the field is growing so rapidly that more individuals are being promoted into supervisory roles. Supervision calls upon a host of skills very different from counseling skills. In addition, there is little training or literature available to help such supervisors acquire and develop these new skills.

Staff Selection Criteria

One of the most important tasks of a supervisor is the hiring of qualified staff members. Precise staff selection criteria must be established prior to the interviewing process. Staff need strong clinical skills in addition to organizational knowledge and training skills.

Criteria may include
- the level of education and academic background needed
- past clinical experience
- knowledge and experience with chemical dependency
- experience in the EAP field
- knowledge of community resources
- ability to communicate with businesses and organizations
- training and presentation skills

Depending on the job responsibilities of the EAP staff, certain criteria may be more relevant than others. Questions based on these criteria should be developed before the actual interview. Similar information can be gathered from all persons interviewed, making the hiring decision more objective. Emphasis should be placed on the skills most needed for the major job responsibilities. At Hazelden, employee assistance counselors are responsible for assessment, referral, and maintenance of company contracts. Therefore, skills in assessment counseling as well as skills that enable counselors to interact with company coordinators — such as communication, presentation, and training skills — are also important.

Initial Orientation and Training for New Staff

After hiring a new staff member, initial orientation is the next supervisory responsibility. Weekly individual meetings with the new staff member are necessary. Helping employees understand the big picture helps to maintain quality service, and thorough orientation and training of a new employee is well-invested time and energy. The time that is spent orienting and teaching a new employee, not only in the tasks necessary for the job, but also in the philosophy and values of the organization and the workers, will more easily integrate new staff members into the work group. The new employee will be able to take on a work load with a minimal amount of confusion and frustration about his or her role and responsibilities.

Training may be accomplished in a variety of ways: observation of fellow staff members, group supervision and case consultation, and individual supervision. Professional workshops and seminars offer a wide range of training opportunities for new and veteran staff. A written staff development plan should be developed and regularly updated.

Supervision

Ongoing supervision of EAP staff includes both *clinical* supervision, issues dealing with clients and cases, and *administrative* supervision, dealing with policies, procedures, and other administrative tasks. An additional task is to help employees set career development plans. As stated earlier, supervision is a difficult challenge and requires a variety of skills. These challenges include learning and maintaining skills in a supervisory role, training and trusting staff to maintain quality services to clients and companies, and meeting the needs of the staff and the organization.

Regularly scheduled individual meetings with staff is a requirement for one-to-one supervision. The frequency (weekly, monthly) will vary with the setting and availability, but the meetings should be scheduled. Allow adequate time to discuss each staff member's successes and difficulties in accomplishing the tasks of his or her job. At these meetings, job expectations should be clear and problems in job performance identified early — before they become a significant performance problem. Goal setting and goal reviewing are other important tasks that need to take place between the supervisor and the staff member.

One of the challenges of the supervisory role is the offering of quality services through line staff. Frequent meetings with individual staff members to discuss case handling will help build the trust that is essential for them to feel comfortable bringing cases and concerns to the supervisor.

Group supervision and case consultation involve regular meetings where much of the actual clinical supervision takes place. All staff are able to help with difficult cases and make suggestions on treatment recommendations. This results in more creative treatment ideas. Working with a multidisciplinary team brings variety to case consultation. Each discipline highlights different aspects of a case and helps assess the case from many perspectives. This wealth of information aids in understanding the case and in developing a treatment plan. Since all staff members have knowledge of different resources, they can expand the possible resource choices for the client.

Case reviews are another mechanism that a supervisor should use to monitor the quality of work done by the staff. Case reviews should be done on a regular basis, and standards for case handling need to be established and communicated to the staff. Selection can be done on a random basis — percentage of cases from each staff member, or a sample from specific types of cases.

Managing EAP Services

Supervisory Style

Supervising a staff of well-trained professionals is difficult at times. They have been trained to be active listeners, to ask appropriate questions, and to request expedient feedback. This is a good situation for building a strong team and good working relationships, but it can also be frustrating. It puts supervisory skills to the test. Certain supervisory styles, such as autocratic or dictatorial ones, do not fit well into this give-and-take relationship. It takes a special blend of offering structure and direction to the job, while allowing freedom for individual flexibility and creativity. A supervisory style needs to be developed and modified depending upon the type of staff and organization in which a supervisor works.

Internships

Some organizations offer internships to students in academic programs. The internship goal is to adequately prepare each trainee for entry level practice as an EAP counselor. Frequent and close supervision of an intern is essential to the successful learning process of the student, even though the primary emphasis is learning by doing. Each intern needs a solid base of knowledge, direction, support, and encouragement from the supervisor. The supervisor should evaluate the student on the development and demonstration of broad-based assessment and motivational counseling skills, and the ability to effectively utilize the community resource network. Close supervision can provide the data for this evaluation. The student needs to feel safe enough, with the support of the supervisor, to branch out and explore the other aspects of the program. He or she should be encouraged to observe and cooperate with many of the other counselors on staff. The student should become involved in all aspects of the program and become an integral part of the staff. Although working with a student may be very time-consuming and difficult, it is exciting to watch a student learn and grow in a supportive learning environment.

The EAP Solution

Self-Care

Self-care for the supervisor is crucial. The work in a supervisory job can become overwhelming. This requires setting realistic limits to maintain a healthy balance between work and private life. Set limits and clear boundaries. Having a well-rounded life experience, both inside and outside the job, will assist in developing a clear perspective of the job. Finding a support group, either inside or outside the organization, can be helpful. It is also often helpful to meet with other supervisors within an organization on a regular basis. A supervisory group outside of the organization is another possibility. Fellow EAP professionals or other therapists in the community may be aware of any such groups. Supervision is a difficult enough challenge; it does not need to be done alone.

Summary

Selecting, training, and supervising new, veteran, and intern staff are the responsibilities of an EAP supervisor. Close supervision is the best assurance that quality services continue to be provided by the counseling staff. There are many new skills that need to be learned and developed, and adequate time to adjust and learn the new position is important. Self-care is essential to maintaining a healthy outlook and perspective on the job. Being a good supervisor is a rewarding and challenging opportunity.

SELECTING AND MONITORING REFERENTS
Richard Selvik, M.S.W., M.P.H.

Richard Selvik manages Hazelden's affiliate network and referral resources. In addition to selecting affiliates he also monitors and evaluates the satisfaction and effectiveness of referrals. He holds master's degrees in public health and social work from the University of Minnesota.

Introduction

Delivering Employee Assistance Program services to large national multisite companies often requires the use of local agencies for in-person assessment, referral, and follow-up services. This section discusses the selection and monitoring of local EAP services to assure uniform services for employees working at different locations for the same company. These affiliates are external EAP service providers that are subcontracted by a national EAP to provide the local services.

The use of affiliates allows large multisite companies to provide a comprehensive EAP for all their employees while avoiding the cost of hiring individuals for each location. Affiliates are knowledgeable about their immediate service delivery area and are familiar with local population characteristics. Contracting with one national EAP to coordinate services reduces the time and costs needed to establish and maintain an affiliate network. For companies that have employees in scattered locations, a telephone referral center can supplement the affiliate network. Generally, if there are fewer than 200 employees at a site, a local provider may not be efficient, but if the national EAP works with several companies, all these local employees can be served by one provider. By keeping affiliates informed about each company they serve, a uniform and comprehensive EAP can be provided to employees.

Selection of Affiliates

There are a variety of chemical dependency and mental health providers across the country who offer EAP services. Because there are many models of EAP service delivery, it is important to find a local affiliate who matches the model of the national contracting EAP. Thus, the same type of service is delivered to all employees and families of the multisite company. This also facilitates comparisons of affiliate service delivery and successful evaluation of the entire program.

Criteria in Selecting Affiliates

Hazelden Employee Assistance Services (EAS) uses standardized criteria and a questionnaire to select affiliates. This questionnaire has evolved over a number of years as Hazelden's affiliate network has grown. Many factors contribute to the selection of an affiliate, including the needs of each Hazelden client company, past experience with the affiliate, legal concerns, chemical dependency expertise, knowledge of EAPs, licensure, and certification. The questionnaire changes as the needs of clients change, the EAP field changes, and mental health/chemical dependency services change. An objective scoring system is used to compare potential affiliates to each other as well as to other affiliates already in the Hazelden affiliate network.

On-site Evaluation

Generally, we have found it necessary to do on-site evaluations rather than telephone interviews. We request a one-month development phase from companies in setting up new affiliates to

- review our resource directory and files on EAP providers in the area
- do the initial phone contacts with local company representatives and EAP providers
- set up appointments
- plan travel schedules
- have a committee review interview results
- select and train the new affiliate so that it is ready to serve the employees and family members in its area.

At Hazelden, we maintain a computerized directory of resources we have used in the past (see the following section on Computerized Resource Lists). Using this data bank we can quickly find potential affiliates. From

Managing EAP Services

this initial background work we usually select three or four prospects to interview, depending on how many EAP providers there are in the area. The interview is conducted with the staff person most likely to be appointed as the affiliate coordinator with Hazelden EAS, the program director, and, in some cases, the agency's executive director.

There are six areas that the interviewer evaluates.

1. *Program Design* — History, organizational structure, services, licensure/credentials, evaluation, confidentiality, hours, telephone answering service, crisis intervention, and malpractice/liability coverage.
2. *Staff Procedures* — Staff size, problem specializations, credentials (if master's level and above), chemical dependency experience (if state has certification, then staff should be certified), staff development, typical cases, intake procedure, documentation, and average length of therapy (for non-EAP work if done).
3. *EAP Experience* — Year begun, current contracts, number of employees, average number of EAP sessions, utilization rate, self vs. supervisory referrals, percentage of problem areas, staff EAP experience, EAP training abilities, and written EAP procedures.
4. *Cost of Service* — Fee per hour and EAP service fee.
5. *Cooperation* — Individual appointed to be coordinator with Hazelden; backup coordinator, who will become familiar with company, knowledge of other resources, ability to refer to other community resources, experience with other resources, and willingness to complete evaluation forms.
6. *Agency Location* — Attractive and accessible physical facilities and proximity to company work site.

During the interview, documentation is collected for later review including general program brochures, resumes, copies of written policies, referral resources used; and licensures, certifications, and insurance coverage on individual staff members and the agency.

Each file on the prospective affiliates is reviewed by a

committee at Hazelden, and a decision is made jointly with the company. Once an affiliate is selected, a training program of Hazelden's EAP procedures and standards is developed.

Monitoring Affiliates

As soon as the first client is seen by an affiliate, monitoring and evaluation begins. Each client is given an orientation information packet explaining how the EAP works and information on the client's rights and responsibilities. An Initial Client Questionnaire and Client Satisfaction Survey is included in this packet. We ask clients to complete it as soon as possible. Also included is a Client Follow-up Permission Form that allows Hazelden to send a questionnaire to their home asking for their impressions of the affiliate after they have used the EAP. The affiliate completes an Assessment/Referral Form on each client seen as well (see Chapter Five in this book on Evaluation and Quality Assurance which covers these forms). Because Hazelden has over 100 affiliates to monitor, we also use site visits and telephone contact to complement the statistical data collected from clients and affiliates.

Computer Monitoring Reports

Hazelden uses a mainframe computer to monitor and evaluate our employee assistance services. Special computer-generated reports are produced on a routine basis to monitor all affiliates.

Any *client record* can be accessed via code number to determine which services have been provided to individual clients. This eliminates the need to keep individual files on the large number of clients seen by any resource. The information collected by affiliates on the Assessment and Referral Form for each client makes up the core data base. The One-Month Follow-Up Form and the External Resource Data Form are linked to each client's Assessment and Referral Form to make up the remainder of the data base from which reports are generated.

Utilization reports are generated for each affiliate just as they are for each company. The utilization report gives us a quick summary of the work each affiliate has done for us over any given time period. Generally, the utilization reports are run quarterly and annually, but they can be run on any time period. It is useful to provide these to affiliates to give them an overview of their work for us. Besides summarizing basic demographic, assessment, and referral information, the utilization report gives us the penetration rate of each affiliate into the total employee population in their area. Particular focus is given to the percentage of management consultation service done, the percentage of supervisor vs. self-referral, and the number of family members who use the EAP. All of this information is useful for developing more company training sessions, mailings, and other efforts to increase employee and family awareness of the EAP.

The utilization report can also be run on all affiliate activity to give an overview of the entire Hazelden network service delivery. From this combined report, service delivery averages are established to compare individual affiliate performance with the overall averages of the network.

To aid analysis of this data, a personal computer is used to generate other reports, graphics, and spread sheets. The personal computer gives us more flexibility to manipulate the data to produce immediate reports or analyses of particular trends. We make extensive use of computer graphics to illustrate trends in service utilization and performance.

The personal computer is also useful in keeping track of smaller data bases of information that are used daily. We keep such a data base on our affiliate network through an *affiliate data sheet* that describes the affiliate's services, staff members, training capabilities, and companies they serve. This data base can generate letters to providers, summarize the affiliate network in any number of ways, as well as keep track of reimbursement rates, last site visits, and contract dates.

Special Evaluation Reports

In order to enhance the service delivery of our affiliate network we have developed specialized evaluation reports that focus on the quality of service. Referral reports provide information about each client such as the dates they were seen, the most significant problem assessed, and where they were referred. From this list, randomly selected cases can be chosen for case reviews. This report also includes a list of affiliate client referrals. This ensures a broad array of local community resources are used, they are appropriate referrals, and more than a few resources are being used by the affiliate (particularly themselves). Our goal is to ensure each client gets an accurate assessment and unbiased referral to the most appropriate resource.

The accurate assessment of alcohol and drug use problems is of particular concern to Hazelden and the EAP field in general. To evaluate this service delivery issue we have developed two *alcohol and drug use assessment reports*. The first report summarizes the A/D assessment rate for each affiliate for employees and family members. The report also breaks the rate down by assessed or most significant problem. A second report lists these data over a three-year period to reveal trends in affiliate activity (i.e., increased or decreased A/D assessment rates). We have taken the data off the mainframe and put it on the personal computer for analysis.

Hazelden has established a benchmark for alcohol and other drug assessment. The 1984 data revealed that as our affiliate network grew, the alcohol and other drug assessment rate dropped. Since that time we have introduced more information on alcohol and other drug assessment to the affiliate network to correct the problem. The rate is slowly coming back up, and we continue to monitor and take action with specific affiliates.

Hazelden continues to develop additional benchmarks of EAP service delivery. Because we offer a broadbrush EAP, we are interested in developing benchmarks for assessment of other problems. We collect data on the assessment of other problems, but because of work force demographics and cultural and geographic differences, it is difficult to set these benchmarks.

Our *follow-up data* is collected via the initial Client Satisfaction Survey and also through a One-Month Follow-Up Questionnaire that is mailed to the clients' homes when they have given us permission to do so. These data are used to respond to clients who were not satisfied with the service one of our affiliates had provided. Clients are called by someone on the Hazelden staff when they indicate on the questionnaire they would like us to call, or when there is any help we can provide over the phone. In some cases they are referred to another resource in their area if they were not happy with our local affiliate. This information is kept on file and if the problem continues, corrective action is taken. We are in the process of computerizing the One-Month Follow-Up Form in order to evaluate each affiliate against benchmarks for client satisfaction of service delivery.

Future developments in the EAP field will lead to new monitoring procedures. Developments such as short-term counseling and preferred provider arrangements, will dictate new ways of evaluating counseling service and the use of local providers for referral. These changes will certainly have impact on the selection and monitoring of affiliates.

Computerized Resource Data Base

Hazelden Employee Assistance Services uses thousands of resources throughout the United States. To keep track of these resources a computerized resource data base has been developed to store a record of each resource and then sort, retrieve, and print out a variety of reports.

Information on resources collected during site visits, over the telephone, or from Hazelden affiliates is recorded on an External Resource Data Form. These forms are similar to the data screens on the mainframe computer into which the data are entered. Numerous pieces of information could be collected on resources. Hazelden selected the data to be collected on the basis of importance and the similarity to other client data. The data also had to be computerizable; some of the items are standardized while others are open-ended.

Resource Data Retrieval

Two preselected data screens and an open-ended data screen can be used for keeping notes (unlimited number of screens) on each resource. These screens are accessed by an identification number that is assigned to each resource when it is entered into the computer. The computer has the capability of creating interrelated subsets of the resources.

Resources can be located through lists generated by the computer. The first list sorts the resources in numerical order and gives the name of the contact person, agency, city, and state of each resource in the computer. Each resource is listed only once on this printout. The second list sorts the resources in alphabetical order based on the keywords of each resource. This list also gives the name of the contact person, agency, city, and state of each resource. It lists each resource as many times as there are keywords for that resource. The third list is the same as the second, except it sorts only the city and state of each resource.

Printed Reports

A One-Month Follow-Up Questionnaire is mailed to clients to evaluate resources, site visits, and telephone contacts. In addition to listing each client's satisfaction with a resource and ability to help in problem resolution, demographic data on each client is provided in an effort to match client with resource. The report is sorted by the provider and by the staff member who referred a client to this resource (we can also sort the list by referral date).

Another report format summarizes data by the number of times we referred someone to a resource, client satisfaction with a resource, or successful resolution of a client's problem. These brief reports allow us to quickly find our most used resources in a certain area and verify our clients' satisfaction with these resources.

Finally, we have created a computer program that allows us to create subdirectories. These smaller directories contain resources that we have designated as belonging to a particular directory. An example of this would be a directory of referents located in an area that covers a number of cities. These directories can be printed out at any time in any of the above report formats.

Not all EAP providers require a computer to manage their services, and many can effectively use one of the many personal computers available. Hazelden's computerized resource directory has evolved over a number of years and will, no doubt, continually be upgraded as new needs arise. The information in the computer also needs to be updated on a daily basis as data on resources change. As often noted, a computerized resource directory is only as good as the data stored in it, and maintaining a computerized directory is critical to its usefulness.

Quality Assurance

Perhaps because of their relatively small staff, lack of external regulation, and short history, EAPs have generally done very little to develop quality assurance programs. However, an increasing amount of self-regulation (credentialing, licensing) within EAP ranks, as well as more external accountability, are increasing the EAP practitioner's interest in evaluation and quality assurance methods.

In this section, examples of quality assurance for Hazelden's Employee Assistance Services will be presented. As compared to other types of evaluation, quality assurance is typically an internal, peer-review process that focuses on service quality. The objectives of a quality assurance program are to 1) establish objective criteria for service quality, 2) monitor actual performance against these criteria, and 3) take corrective action when performance is below expectations.

Our approach in developing quality assurance standards was to involve staff in developing reasonable and measurable standards. We also emphasized flexibility by having ranges of performance, rather than a single target. Our standards are intentionally simple and flexible. And the goal is to improve overall quality of care. Hazelden's EAP quality standards include outcome measures to assess what we do and our results.

Since 1979, Hazelden has provided contracted EAP services to diverse local and multisite national employers. As staff and contracts grew, the need for uniformity in services, standards, and monitoring became apparent. As an organization, Hazelden has a formal quality assurance function with Board involvement, and it was appropriate to include our EAP services in this system.

A quality assurance group, consisting of EAP counseling, administrative, and supervisory staff, conducted a series of monthly meetings to identify a development strategy and implement the quality assurance procedures. In our view, the ultimate success of the process depended on doing the right things in the right order. This process not only aided service quality, but also improved employee support for the end product.

The first task of the team was to review and modify the department's overall mission statement. Following agreement on the written mission, two meetings focused on the development of a values and philosophy statement. The service model, primarily assessment and referral counseling utilizing both a national network of in-person counselors, as well as a 24-hour Helpline, was reviewed and affirmed.

Finally, the team's major emphasis became the development of service objectives, brief procedures statements, and performance standards for eight areas of EAP service areas: Program Implementation, Administrative Support, EAP Counseling, Contract Management, Staff Development, Program Communications, EAP Training, and Evaluation. A service manual summarizing key elements of the above process was then published and distributed to all staff as a training and reference vehicle. This product is updated on an ongoing basis to reflect changes in both services and standards.

Data from our management information system, and employee and client surveys are all used to monitor performance. For a more complete discussion of possible standards see Donald Jones, *Performance Benchmarks for the Comprehensive Employee Assistance Program*, (Hazelden Educational Materials, 1983). A formal, written procedure for addressing complaints or problems was also developed. Case reviews are routinely conducted by the counselors using a random sample of open and closed cases. But a major emphasis has been on client data. (The next section contains a brief overview of EAP service standards as an example of EAP quality assurance.)

A major emphasis of the EAP QA program has been the monitoring of client follow-up data from a one-month questionnaire, mailed to all in-person clients one month after the last scheduled EAP session. (See a sample of the questionnaire in the Appendix.)

The performance benchmarks listed in Figure 4 were derived from historical experience and influenced by both management and employee interest in maximizing service quality. Despite some fluctuation each quarter, most standards are met or exceeded. A range of acceptable outcomes, rather than a fixed percentage, help convey the understanding that there is no single right answer but acceptable levels of performance. Those standards which are not consistently met are reviewed. For example, it appears that the problem improvement standard may be high for a model that focuses on assessment and referral rather than direct treatment. Also, the length of time allowed for problem change may not be sufficient as many clients have just started treatment at a community resource when they receive the EAP client questionnaire. Following completion of Hazelden EAS in the future, comparative data will be gathered at different time intervals to help establish an appropriate standard.

In the meantime, EAS has developed and implemented a more timely measure of client satisfaction. A Client Satisfaction Survey is administered to each client at his or her first visit as part of the Client Orientation Kit (which includes statements of confidentiality, client rights, and a follow-up permission form). Each client is asked to return the survey immediately following completion of EAP counseling. This allows timely and more personalized feedback on client satisfaction and provides an early opportunity to correct service problems.

A quality assurance system should also include data from the EAP's information system, surveys, case reviews, and complaints or problems. The most critical element is a commitment to take corrective action and improve quality.

As the EAP field evolves, quality assurance will become more significant in demonstrating and improving quality. New EAP models focusing on cost-containment, short-term counseling, and health promotion, will require new standards. At this time, many of these new models are being developed and implemented by the newest member of the EAP team — the marketing department — the subject of our next chapter.

Figure 4
Hazelden EAP Quality Assurance Standards

Client-Reported Satisfaction With:	**Quality Assurance Benchmarks**
Response time to see an EAP counselor	90 – 95%
Concern shown by the EAP counselor	90 – 95%
Confidentiality of the EAP contact	90 – 95%
Effectiveness of the EAP contact	85 – 90%
Overall *satisfaction* with the EAP	85 – 90%
Client-Reported Experience With the Referral:	
Received a referral from the EAP	75 – 80%
Contacted the referral given by the EAP	75 – 80%
Satisfied with the referral received from the EAP	75 – 80%
Overall, the original *problem has improved*	70 – 75%

3

MARKETING
Gary Hestness and Vincent Hyman

Gary Hestness is the Manager of Outreach for Hazelden and has been involved in EAP marketing and sales since 1976. A graduate of the University of Minnesota, Gary also teaches in Hazelden workshops and has helped develop employee assistance programs nationally and internationally. Vince Hyman is a writer for Hazelden's Outreach Department and develops and writes a variety of promotional materials for employee assistance and other services.

Introduction

In the early days of employee assistance, most programs were focused on occupational alcoholism. The marketing of these programs was done by a recovering alcoholic or family member who was committed to helping his or her fellow employees. As the results of these efforts grew, the word spread that alcoholism is a disease and recovery is possible. Federal funding was made available to train employee assistance program professionals and to help other organizations start their own program.

The EAP Solution

The evolution of the broadbrush program is described in other chapters; in this chapter it will be discussed from a marketing perspective. Many people were, and are, helped by the occupational alcoholism program, but the broadbrush EAP had a larger appeal to many employers. As the concept grew, other types of professionals came into the field — social workers, psychologists, and even salespeople.

It would not be fitting to talk about marketing EAPs without mentioning a marketing technique used in the state of Minnesota in the mid-1970s. The idea was presented to Governor Wendell Anderson by a group of prominent chemical dependency professionals. These professionals were asked to spend three days in a think tank to develop ideas on how to identify people who had personal problems that could develop into job performance problems. In addition, it was decided that a target for the project would be small employers. Their idea was to establish agencies throughout Minnesota to sell the concept of employee assistance to small businesses of up to 200 employees. There were incentives: the first year 90 percent of the cost was paid by the state, the second year 50 percent, and the third year 10 percent. Along with this, the state picked up the initial consulting and training costs. During the years of this "Governor's Bill," over 1,000 corporate programs were developed, and EAP providers were established. Large companies also began to look at the model of broadbrush EAP and the option of contracting with professional off-site providers. These large companies were not eligible for reimbursement by the state. However, the consulting agency did receive a development or start-up fee if an organization with over 200 employees started a program.

Employee assistance programs are still changing and evolving, and marketing strategies must adapt to these changes. As the corporate world becomes more knowledgeable, new questions are being asked. Most companies understand an EAP from a human resources perspective. It makes good sense to identify troubled employees and offer them the opportunity to help themselves. Many understand that if you fire someone because of poor job performance caused by a personal problem, there is no guarantee the next person you hire will not have the same performance problems. It is difficult to screen out emotional problems or alcoholism during the employment interview. Corporate America is now beginning to ask new questions: "How will I know if you can really save me money?" "Are the referrals you make cost effective, and will this service increase my health care costs?" The answers are clearly the marketing and sales issues of the future. While the EAP concept can still be sold on its intuitive merits, it will no longer be possible to sell or maintain programs without measurable results.

The new health care industry also poses many questions for the EAP field. Will preferred provider arrangements exclude the EAP professional, or will it include the EAP in the model? How will the growing Health Maintenance Organization (HMO) movement affect EAPs? Fewer social services are available to an ever-growing population. Private industry has been asked to take on more of the burden in terms of financial support and service provision, and the workplace is now a new frontier for social service professionals. Marketing is critical in helping the EAP build on past successes and meet future needs.

Overview

Marketing involves a broad range of functions such as developing promotional materials and media relations, including newspaper, radio, TV ads, direct sales, and the integration of the four Ps — product, price, place, and promotion—into the strategic plan of an organization.

Without a plan and specific measurable goals, marketing can be a costly and ineffective process. Too often, marketing programs are not well planned or comprehensive. They often focus only on advertising and the results are disappointing.

Human services have given little support to the marketing function. Asking someone with eight to ten years of clinical counseling training to do the marketing for a human service agency is like asking an advertising professional to do family systems therapy — the results in both cases will speak for themselves. If an EAP or any other human service is to grow, it's necessary to provide the resources for successful marketing.

In the remainder of this chapter we will review some of the key components of an EAP marketing program beginning with the product and the customer.

Determining the Product and the Customer

Earlier sections have described the range of services (products) encompassed in the concept of employee assistance programs. But from a marketing perspective the central issue is not what services the EAP can deliver, but rather what services the customer wants. In most cases employers are the customers, and they have a variety of needs — humanistic, economic, and fiduciary. Employers (or the union) may see the EAP as a demonstration of their commitment to the well-being of employees and families, as a cost-savings tool, as a way of improving supervisory effectiveness, as a legal obligation to provide health care or reduce industrial accidents, or all of these. Historically, employee assistance programs have been close to the customer. The first EAPs were in-house programs and delivered only those services the employer wanted. External EAPs are also strongly market-driven, and *it is this marketing orientation that accounts to a great extent for the diversity and the success of employee assistance programs*. (EAPs have also been relatively free from other factors that typically limit a marketing orientation in the health care fields — regulation, licensing, and control by professional associations.) EAPs have quickly applied the concept of segmentation by developing alternate EAP models for a diverse marketplace. Therefore, it would be misleading in a chapter on marketing to define what services an EAP should offer. Rather, the marketing concept requires the EAP professional (whether in-house or external) to determine what needs the customer has and how the EAP can meet these.

The EAP has other customers in addition to the employer, sponsor, or union; these are the clients, employees, and families receiving direct services. Training, communication materials, and counseling are the essential services of an EAP and should be considered from a marketing perspective. "Are the clients' needs being met?" is more than a clinical question, and the EAP staff should recognize that through their interactions with clients they are conveying an image about the EAP that can make or break the EAP. This duality of clients and buyers is one of the unique aspects of health care marketing. It will become even more complex as new customers such as PPOs, HMOs, and insurance companies enter the scene. A comprehensive marketing plan will address not only how to gain the support of the employer, but also how to keep the support of clients and others involved in the EAP.

The product provided by an EAP is a service, and interpersonal relationships are the primary component. Attention should be focused on the nature of these interactions. The skills and competencies of the EAP staff are clearly part of the product (Goldman, et al., 1984:94). Employers will expect the EAP staff to be trained, experienced professionals who provide effective services.

In developing EAP services, the planner should focus on customer needs and the benefits of the EAP. Although the EAP has the flexibility to adapt to the needs of a diverse and changing marketplace, no employee assistance program can be all things to all people. A successful marketing program is more than product development. The next sections will focus on the other components of EAP marketing.

Place

At first glance, the concept of place seems more appropriate for the marketing of tangible products. However, for services, place may be one of the most significant marketing variables. *For the EAP, place can be interpreted as availability, accessibility, and confidentiality.* The company and the client will want services that are available when needed and that are easily accessible and confidential. Careful consideration should be given to staffing patterns, office hours, office locations, and telephone coverage to maximize the EAP's ability to be there when needed. And confidentiality should not only be promoted, but assured through explicit and monitored policies and procedures.

For Hazelden this has meant the development of the 24-hour, toll-free telephone system, several office locations, and the use of local affiliates to provide in-person counseling where we do not have Hazelden EAP counselors. The management of this system has necessitated having specialized staff who use computerized information to assure our service standards are being met. This area requires constant attention because it is difficult to meet all the customer's needs for accessibility within the available financial resources. A key marketing issue is to be careful not to promise more than you can deliver. Counselors miss work, telephones fail, and receptionists mishandle appointments. A dynamic tension exists between the customer's wants and the staff's ability to meet them. Therefore, it is important to spend time during the sales process clarifying what the customer wants and how you will meet these needs. Many of our evaluation measures focus on these areas, and routine monitoring can help spot problems before the contract is jeopardized.

Promotional Techniques

Promotion is the communications mechanism of marketing. The goal of promotion is to inform and persuade your consumers to respond to the service you are offering. We tend to think of promotion as advertising, but advertising is just one of many tools available to you as you promote your EAP. Marketers think of promotion as a mix of various tools, ranging from word-of-mouth news about your service to extensive use of radio, television, print, and direct mail advertising. Generally, we divide these tools into four basic categories:

- personal sales
- mass sales (advertising)
- publicity (news coverage about your service)
- sales promotion (special offers, coupons, and similar devices)

Marketing

The term *promotional mix* describes the way you use these four elements as you promote your services. While all the elements are available to the EAP marketer, the complexity and expense of employee assistance require extensive personal contact simply to explain the service, let alone close a sale. Other promotional techniques, such as print and broadcast media, advertising, direct mail, informational brochures, and publicity, are used to support the actual sales contact. In contrast, marketers of soft drinks rely heavily on advertising and sales promotions to generate a sale; they have almost no contact with the final consumer.

Later in this chapter, we will discuss the mechanics of personal selling. This section will focus on the development of a message or image to represent your EAP and the consistent use of that message in promoting your service.

Developing an Image

Employee assistance is a long-term business. You cannot sell a contract and walk away; the program must be carefully managed for years. Therefore, your communications must consistently deliver the same message before the sale, during the sale, and throughout service delivery. That message — your image — must reflect who you are and who you want to reach.

Before developing any promotional materials, you should begin with a comprehensive audit of your service. Ask yourself these questions:

- Do we have a mission statement? What does it say?
- Is our EAP local, regional, or national?
- What size businesses do we serve best?
- Who is our target audience within those businesses? (In small companies, you may speak directly to the owner; in larger organizations, your audience may be human resource managers, benefits managers, or the resident occupational alcoholism counselor.)
- Why are we in the EAP business? Are we part of a larger health agency, or an independent EAP?

The EAP Solution

- Who is our competition? What do they have to offer, and what differentiates us from them?
- What are our key benefits and strengths? Why do our customers choose to do business with us?
- What makes us unique? Do we offer in-depth knowledge of local resources, an understanding of federal bureaucracies, a small staff with a personal touch, a large, nationwide system with regional centers and sophisticated management, or a special understanding of factory environments?

Your answers to these questions will help you formulate a written statement of your position in the EAP marketplace. As you develop promotional materials, you can check them against this *position statement*.

After creating a position statement, the next step is to develop a body of promotional materials to convey and reinforce that position.

Developing Promotional Materials

In developing a body of promotional materials you will also develop a specific *identity* for your EAP. By identity, we mean a visual appearance that is immediately recognizable to your clients, their employees, and hopefully, your potential customers.

If your organization is a part of a larger hospital or health service delivery system, corporate identity guidelines may already exist. These guidelines specify the ways in which your logo, typefaces, printed materials, color choices, brochures and newsletter formats, and signatures may be used.

If your EAP is new or is creating its own identity, you may need to hire an agency to create an identity for you. At the minimum, this will include

- a logo design
- stationery
- business cards
- a brochure describing your services
- guidelines for creating future promotional items.

Other items you may want to include are

- a "white paper" or technical description of your services
- leaflets to mail to employees

- posters to be placed at your clients' sites
- fact sheets on your history, sample policy statement, and staff resumes
- a folder to hold it all together

All of these elements work together to reinforce your identity. For example, a potential client may first see your employee poster at a colleague's business site. He or she may call, requesting information. You respond with a letter, enclosing a brochure. Later, your prospect may spot your ad in a local trade magazine. By the time you prepare to make a sales presentation, the potential client has already developed a subconscious feeling about your services, based on your visual identity. The materials you use throughout your sales presentation — folder, fact sheets, sample employee leaflets — continue to reinforce that identity. The end result for your audience is a sense of confidence about the consistency of your service.

Of course, your final goal is to sell a contract and to follow up with excellent service. No matter how impressive your sales materials are, they cannot make a sale. But consistent, attractive materials do serve notice that you are serious about your business.

Visual Aids

When dealing with an intangible service like an EAP, the more the concept can be brought to life, the better. In most cases, the salesperson is the only representative a company ever sees, and the decision is usually based on the impression this professional makes. Regarding sales strategy: If possible, bring in your experts — counselors, research specialists, or treatment team people. There is value in the special skills of the expert. Of course, the expert has to have business experience and must be able to communicate in a language understandable to the prospect.

Sales presentations use four types of visual aids: overhead transparencies, slides, videotapes, and flip charts. Each technology has advantages and disadvantages. Overheads work well with both small and large groups. Then ask yourself, "What do I want the visual to accomplish?" "Should it be an outline for the presenter, highlight a point, or make a statement?" Some basic rules are: Have no more than three points per overhead. Use the overhead to highlight a point, not to describe it in detail. Graphs and charts can be effective if you have a handout to accompany your overhead. An overhead usually cannot be used to convey feelings.

Slides can have more impact on a motivational and feeling level. You can make a presentation with the same content with or without slides (e.g., people in different stages of counseling), but the impact will be greater with the slides. Organizations do not buy EAPs, people do, and usually because of an emotional connection to the service side of the program. Of course, this is not always true, but even those who buy for purely financial reasons will pull out if there is not sufficient evidence that people are getting help. Slides can be viewed with groups of from ten to 500 and more, but with very small numbers, some of the flow is lost. It is easy to get carried away with a long impressive show using 50 or 60 slides. Be respectful of the decision makers' time. Use fewer slides and stress the most important points. Use the old phrase "sell the sizzle, not the steak." Do not confuse your audience with every technical aspect of the counseling or referral process. Keep it simple.

One of the newest tools to be used is the videotape. This can be used with large or small audiences. You can be sure all the key information will be given in a videotape. People are accustomed to the TV screen, and it is a friendly way of transmitting information. The big advantage with video is it can stand alone. If people miss your presentation, they can easily see it later or replay it as a refresher. But videotapes are expensive to produce and are not as entertaining as in-person presentations.

Finally, flip charts can help give an organized, professional-looking presentation. Group size can be small or large. This type of visual is an excellent guide for the presenter. The one disadvantage is that your talk can appear "canned" and may not address the specific needs of the target group.

Marketing

Advertising

We have already discussed the importance of developing a position statement and creating an identity that reflects your position, as well as the role of sales support materials and visual aids in reinforcing your identity. For many employee assistance providers, this is sufficient — or it may represent realistic budget limitations.

However, advertising can be a powerful tool as you create and build your identity in the minds of your target audience. Compared to personal sales calls, advertising is very cost-efficient in terms of cost per contact, but it can be expensive to produce and place ads.

The most important factor in developing advertisements is your target audience. This relates to the position statement you have already developed. Advertisers choose media in which to place ads by determining which medium the target audience is most likely to see and hear. The combination of various forms of advertising available — television, radio, print, billboards, direct mail — is called a *media mix*; the schedule for placement in these media is called a *media plan*.

For most EAPs, the media mix can be built on a combination of print and direct mail. If you have positioned yourself carefully, there are usually a number of readily available trade magazines for ad placements and mailing lists for direct mail pieces.

If, for example, you have specified manufacturing companies of less than 500 employees as your target audience, you can locate trade magazines, newsletters, and other print pieces likely to be read by your prospects. You can also rent mailing lists that include those prospects.

In contrast to print and direct mail, the production costs of television and radio advertising are very high. However, the cost per contact is much lower, because broadcast media reach so many people. And with the availability of special programming for business news programs, you may be able to make good use of these media.

The decision to advertise is a difficult one. It should be made after careful consideration of your available resources. If you decide to advertise, you will want to choose a good advertising agency or consultant to guide you through this complex industry. And you should be prepared to spend enough money to make your efforts worthwhile.

Purchasing Creative Services

Unless you have staff specializing in designing and writing promotional materials, you will need to hire an outside consultant. This may mean an advertising agency, or a combination of free-lance writers, designers, photographers, and other creative vendors. Regardless of the type of outside services you need, there are two factors to consider:

- the quality of similar materials produced by the vendors in question
- the prices charged for various services

Here are some guidelines to help you in purchasing creative services.

- Examine samples of the vendor's previous work. Does it communicate clearly? Does it convey a message of quality? What marketing problem was addressed in each sample? How creative and effective were the solutions?
- Get a list of references and call them. Were projects completed on time and within budget? Did the vendor show exceptional skill as a problem solver? Did the vendor behave professionally, keep appointments, and demonstrate a good understanding of the client's needs?
- Look for experience with businesses similar to yours. Does the vendor understand human services? Does the vendor understand your target audiences? If not, does the vendor show flexibility in working with a wide range of clients? Is the vendor a fast learner?
- Look for examples of work similar to the project you are working on. If you need only a simple brochure, steer away from vendors that specialize in elaborate advertising campaigns. If you need a logo and corporate identity program, look for vendors with that experience. Many vendors specialize in different areas.

- Be specific about exactly what you need. Provide the vendor with a list of your needs and expected completion dates.
- Listen to how the vendor communicates. Does the vendor try to discover your needs? Do you sense a rapport? Will you enjoy working with the vendor?

If you have never purchased creative services, plan on interviewing at least six vendors. Make careful notes as you interview and ask each to submit a detailed proposal and cost estimate within a specified time frame. Judge the estimates on all of this criteria, not just price. And before you make a final decision, ask to see the vendor's facility. A tour can tell you a lot about the quality of service you will receive.

Writing Proposals

At some stage in working with private industry and in most negotiations with public agencies, the EAP will need to submit a written proposal. Although the proposal stage is part of the sales process, preparing a proposal is not the same as writing a promotional piece. A proposal is intended to demonstrate your capability to deliver services at a specified price. The organization issuing the request for a proposal has already decided to have an EAP and knows what services are needed — you need to convince them you can do the job. This is in contrast to a written promotion that often is intended to educate or persuade the reader and elicit interest.

Excellent books have been written about proposal development, and many organizations offer training in this area (see the References and Appendixes). Some specific suggestions based on our experience (and mistakes) are

- Assign someone in your organization to look for proposals listed in state and federal registries (such as Commerce Business Daily).
- If you decide to pursue proposal writing, spend some time and money training someone in your organization in proposal writing *and* how to manage the proposal preparation and submission process.

The EAP Solution

- Do not overwrite a proposal. You are not trying to sell the reader on the idea of an EAP; you are trying to establish your capability. Present your services in an objective, factual manner.
- Do your homework. Find out as much as possible about the organization issuing the proposal, how it will be reviewed, and who will review the proposal. (Federal and other governmental agencies have specific guidelines on the release of information about proposals. Make sure you understand these guidelines and do not violate them.)
- Submit the proposal on time.
- Address all points in the proposal clearly and visibly. Leave little to the reviewers' imagination. Follow the requester's outline.
- Write a precise proposal and use a plain brown wrapper; extra length and fancy packaging aren't the criteria.
- Make sure the sales staff understand the proposal since a salesperson may be invited to the final oral interview.
- If you do not get the contract, request a follow-up interview to determine what factors were seen as weaknesses in the proposal. With federal contracts you may request a copy of the winning proposal.

Direct Sales

What motivates a person or a company to buy employee assistance services? Most people have strong opinions about their company's productivity and its relationship with its employees. To begin the sales process, one must learn what motivates any particular organization and then guide them in discovering how the EAP can best solve their problems. Employers may say, "We want to reduce turnover; there are too many grievances; safety is the big problem here; this company must reduce its costs and increase its productivity." Other key phrases are, "This company has always been a leader in our community; the welfare of our employees is an important part of our company's success."

The role of direct sales in the marketing of an EAP is vital to developing new programs. There are two

Marketing

reasons for this. First, an EAP is an intangible product. The perception of the value of an EAP differs widely among the potential customers. Some feel it is a fine way to communicate the trust and cooperation between management and labor. On the other end of the scale, some would consider these programs an excellent way to identify and eliminate poor performers. It takes a salesperson to discover what customers want and to help them solve their problems. This is what direct selling can do — identify needs and solve problems. To many in the human services field, this may sound familiar. There are many similarities between selling and counseling (Wilson, 1978). Some of the key elements in counseling include empathy, good listening skills, ability to develop trust, genuineness, concreteness, and the ability to identify a problem and motivate the client to take action to resolve his or her difficulty. These same principles apply to the salesperson who works with a prospective client.

An organization called Wilson Learning Center in Bloomington, Minnesota, offers a course called "Counselor Selling" (see References) that uses traditional selling principles combined with accepted practices in the counseling field. The combination of these two disciplines seems to be a good match for the human service field that must now learn to sell its services.

In the Wilson Learning terminology, there are four basic components in the sales process: building trust, finding the client's needs, developing commonality, and closing the sale (Wilson, 1978). Counselor selling is a process just like client counseling; these four stages are interdependent and must be followed to gain the most effective outcome. Phase one is *relating*. In this stage, building trust is the goal. This can be accomplished in many ways, but developing commonality and expressing intent are important. Make sure you dress appropriately for the business and setting. In a bank or a corporate headquarters, a business suit and basic conservative dress is the most appropriate. Stop by the organization you are planning to call on and ask for their corporate report and the correct title and name of the person you are meeting. This will give you an idea

The EAP Solution

of the setting and dress of the people. Intent is also a factor. It is important to convey the message that you are there to help the company solve its problems. An approach could include, "I have no idea if you need our service. I am interested in finding out how you currently deal with productivity and employee problems." With this approach, you set the stage as a problem solver rather than a salesperson.

The second phase is called *discovery*. In this situation, you determine your prospect's needs. Is the company satisfied with its turnover rate, current level of productivity, quality of its product or service, current use of its medical plan, absenteeism, or general attitude of employees about their company? Any or all of these areas could be used to identify needs. Bring out concerns each organization has, but do not assume you know the answer. The questions can then be directed at current attempts to improve or change the situation. This will give you an idea of the spread between what the prospect has and what is needed.

The next phase is *advocating*. Be sure you agree on the problem as perceived by the customer, and he or she wants to solve it. With this agreement, you can then proceed with possible solutions. You are no longer a salesperson, but a counselor and problem solver. Look at the amount of change desired and develop methods to measure the results.

Once the problem has been agreed upon and a commitment obtained from the prospect that change is desired, the process of *supporting* can begin or, in the language of sales, "closing." The close has been viewed by many as a time of stress, arm-twisting, and high-pressure tactics. The difference in the Wilson model is that "closing" is not a forced decision, but a stage where the salesperson supports the client in making a decision that solves problems and meets the client's needs.

There are three other sales techniques that are worth mentioning: prospecting, the use of the telephone, and the use of research. Volumes have been written about *prospecting* and its importance. It cannot be emphasized enough that development of a systematic and consistent method is necessary to conduct this task. Prospecting should always be ongoing. The theory behind this is called the *pipeline theory*. Simply stated, selling is a process that has many stages. If one concentrates on just one phase, such as closing the sale, the pipeline will dry up because no new prospects have been developed. Prospecting is systematic, and goals are set as to the number of calls to make per day. These calls, in turn, will net a certain number of callbacks, appointments, and requests for information. Every call is important, and accurate records will pay off in the long run.

How does prospecting happen? First, the specific market must be targeted. Will you look for large companies, small companies, local or multisite national companies, public sector or private, and is there a specific kind of organization you want to work with? Then there are some reality checks. What is the economy doing to certain industries? Who is making money right now? Five years ago, the oil and gas companies were doing well and were looking at expanding their benefits to employees. Today, the auto industry has started making more inquiries about EAPs. One must be sensitive to these trends. Once the target is identified, there are many resources to help locate the company and its offices. The public library is at the top of the list. You can find corporate reports, references such as *Dun and Bradstreet, Standard and Poors,* and *The Wall Street Journal.* Look for trade shows that feature the preferred industries or key buyers such as human resource associations or management consulting groups. Prospects are also organizations you do business with. In Minnesota, a group of corporations called the Five Percenters contribute five percent of their pretax earnings to charity. These organizations have a high social conscience and image in the community, and they have been responsive to the concept of employee assistance. Once a large contract is signed, this can also be a key factor in prospecting. Organizations talk to each other, and they learn what others are doing. Referrals to other organizations by your clients can produce big benefits not only in approaching a new prospect, but because your work with a respected firm gives your program automatic credibility. The method of finding companies can range from using the public library to talking with your next-door neighbor. The basic idea of prospecting is that without it nothing else can happen.

Telemarketing is a learned skill. There are two parts to the use of the phone: psychology and skill building. One problem for many people is "call reluctance" or a fear of rejection. There is little one can say about this fear, other than making calls regularly desensitizes that anxiety. Interestingly enough, telephone practice on a regular basis develops the skills necessary to do it well. There is a rule of thumb about calling for EAPs: It is difficult to sell the concept or individual components over the telephone. An EAP is an intangible product; the process of developing trust, commonality, discovering, advocating, and supporting, is not done by telephone. The most important point is to sell the appointment, not the product. Give the person choices of times and places to meet, not whether or not to buy an EAP. Calling someone you do not know (cold calls) and trying to start up a conversation is not easy for anyone. There are two principles to follow: One, the call is a conversation with a purpose. You want to stimulate enough interest to get an appointment. Two, you must understand the numbers game. If ten calls are made, the probability of getting two appointments is very good. As the salesperson develops new confidence and skill, the probability will increase.

Research data can be a tool to help generate interest or close a sale. Chief executive officers and managers are always looking for ways to make better decisions, and EAP research can give them that ability. Just having access to research can make a difference. This field has been selling programs on the humanistic value of EAPs, but a cost-benefit approach will have to be developed to maintain them through good and hard times.

EAP Sales as a Process

There are two important elements in the EAP sales process: choosing the right time to close the sale and determining the right person to contact. Closing a sale starts with the very first call. A number of steps have been described in the sales process from building trust to advocating for a decision. Closing a sale is an attitude, an ability to know when to ask for a commitment. Usually many small decisions have already been made by the customer. The first decision was to see the salesperson. Next, a decision was made about the needs of the particular company. Asking questions and getting agreement that your prospect wants to solve identified problems are keys to the close. Once all these small closing steps are followed, it is time to use traditional sales techniques. The 80/20 rule is widely used in sales. This rule states that most decisions are made when a deadline is identified. Eighty percent of the serious negotiations happen in the last twenty percent of the time remaining. These can be structured around a price change, a special offer, or a proposal which guarantees prices for 90 days. Another technique is to not ask for the sale, but for the time when a decision will be made about the sale.

Closing the sale is not possible unless you are talking to the right person — the decision maker. How does the salesperson know if he or she is talking to the decision maker? If you are talking to the president or the chief executive officer, you are talking to the decision maker. This is always the best place to start, even if the president or CEO does not have the time to see you. If this person refers you to someone else, it will have a powerful impact on whoever you do see. The larger the company, the more difficult it is to see the top person. The responsibility usually falls in the area of human resources or the medical department. Other areas might include the training department, industrial relations, or the safety area. Other departments can have an interest if they are experiencing problems or an individual within a department takes a special interest in this area. The challenge is to find your support. With the larger companies, group presentations are often the method used to present EAP information. It gives the presenter a chance to expose the concept to a broad range of people.

The EAP Solution

Pricing Strategies

Pricing decisions should be based on financial, marketing, and service quality factors. Financial decisions basically rely on expectations — not meeting all expenses, breaking even, or generating a surplus of revenues over expenses within a defined time period. Before you begin marketing EAPs, a careful cost-finding study should be completed to determine the price required to meet your financial target. Marketing decisions typically focus on how to price the EAP in order to acquire the contract — and this price may be higher or lower than the financial target determined through the cost-finding study. Perhaps most important, the EAP should determine its quality of service standards. For example, the level of service can be reduced to lower the price in a competitive marketplace, but the EAP should know the service "bottom line" in order to protect the integrity of the program. Some of the more common pricing strategies are shown in Figure 5.

Doing a cost-finding study for an EAP is similar to that of any other health or social service. All direct costs should be identified, indirects added, the break-even point determined, and the desired surplus included. As the volume of EAP business increases, there may be per unit cost reductions as administrative, training, and other costs stabilize. However, the major cost of counselor time will tend to be directly correlated to the number of clients seen and will increase steadily with new business. It is impossible to provide much specific information for the reader on cost-finding since each EAP will have a different array of services and therefore very different costs. But a point to remember is for every hour that a counselor sees a client there is easily another hour spent on documentation, contact with referrals, and related activities. Early in the development of Hazelden's EAP we kept detailed time logs to generate data for cost finding, and this approach is recommended for the beginning program. (We also stopped keeping the logs once we had the information, since there was a cost associated with the log system which either had to be passed on to the customer or be considered a developmental cost to be paid out of future revenues.)

Marketing

Figure 5
Pricing Strategies

Type	Definition	Advantages	Disadvantages
Loss leader	Pricing a service or product at a loss under the assumption that along with this product the customer will make additional purchases that cover the loss.	True loss leaders can be very effective in increasing overall sales.	Often confused with subsidized pricing with the result that the costs of the loss leader are never recovered.
Subsidized	Using revenue from other areas to offset the true cost of a service to allow the service to be sold at a lower rate.	Best if seen as a short-term method of entering a new market. A form of cost shifting. Allows an organization to provide needed services that are not profitable.	In the long run, the subsidized services can drain resources needed for other services or diversification.
Penetration	Setting a price that is below competitors in order to enter a new market.	Can be used to get into a competitive product or service line where you are unknown.	Assumes that price is an important motivator for consumers. Cannot be sustained since losses will increase.
Controlled	Pricing at a rate imposed by an external agent.	Advantages accrue to providers able to maintain a surplus for growth.	Does not allow for diversification. Associates high costs of regulation.
Competitive	Setting a price that is comparable to competitors.	May be essential to keep market share, if price is a major factor in consumer's buying behavior.	Has no necessary relationship to profitability. Requires a good knowledge of the competition's services and prices.
Margin-based	Pricing at a level that results in a desired return-on-investment or surplus.	Assures that revenue and profitability goals are met.	Requires good cost accounting. Has no necessary relationship to the marketplace, can be too high or too low. Mistakes in projecting volume can invalidate the pricing.
Skim-pricing	Pricing a service or product at a very high level to skim off the initial business.	Very effective in generating revenue when the market is unlikely to last.	A short-term strategy. The service must be unique and the market short-lived.
Penalty	Setting a price high enough to discourage customers unable to afford the service or product.	Highly profitable. Allows you to control your customer mix.	Can give you an image of expensive or elitist. Later expansion into other markets or customer groups can be difficult.
Feels-good	Relying on tradition, precedent, intuition, what feels good.	Requires no analysis, cost finding, or market research.	You won't know you're wrong until it's too late.

SOURCE: Spicer, 1985

The EAP Solution

The marketing issues are more complex. Marketing staff should provide information on prices being charged by competitors *for similar services* and how price sensitive the marketplace is. Most likely the marketplace will be very price sensitive since employers are increasingly concerned about health care cost containment. Prices charged by competitors will vary from free to $40. (Typical current prices in Hazelden's market appear to range from twelve dollars to twenty dollars per employee, per year. However, some programs offer free EAP services, and lower-priced programs are sold at about six dollars to eight dollars. We assume these less expensive EAP providers have taken a "loss leader," "subsidized," or "penetration" pricing approach.)

The third factor in deciding price is service quality. Marketing staff will try to offer as much service as possible at the lowest possible price since that is exactly what the buyer wants. The finance officer will want to assure attainment of the financial target. Trying to cope with these sometimes divergent philosophies requires a commitment to maintaining the basic integrity of the EAP. This commitment should be based on specific, measurable standards to avoid conflict over vague philosophical concerns. Without these standards, the EAP will be in danger of delivering too little service with the probable result of customer dissatisfaction and loss of business and public image.

Finally, a note on the other customer — the client. A core philosophy of the EAP has been that the client or employee is never charged for EAP services (we often say that it is free, but like all employee benefits it is not free, only not billed). By not charging for the EAP services, employees are encouraged to seek help and utilize the program. Charging for EAP services could decrease utilization and acceptance of the program, at least in theory. Given the current trend of passing more of the cost of medical benefits to employees (i.e., cafeteria benefit plans) we can anticipate that someone may elect to charge employees for EAP use. In the author's opinion, this will drastically harm the nature of the EAP.

Marketing

Reimbursement Models

Once the price has been determined, the next decision is how the EAP vendor will be reimbursed. Typically, EAPs are prepaid on a per capita, annual basis assuming a given level of utilization (e.g., $20 per employee per year). This approach puts the EAP provider at risk since services must be delivered even if demand exceeds projections, unless the fee can be adjusted depending on utilization. Cost of other services such as training, communications, or reporting may be included in the per employee fee or "unbundled" and paid separately. The disadvantage of charging separately for services is the buyer may elect not to have these services and limit the comprehensiveness and effectiveness of the EAP, which may then be seen as a performance deficit of the vendor. In our experience this is particularly true of training purchased only for the first year, with the result that newly hired employees and supervisors are not trained and utilization of the EAP decreases to the dismay of both the employer and the EAP.

EAP reimbursement can also be on a fee-for-service model based on actual services delivered. This is less risky for the vendor, but increases administrative overhead as more records must be kept to prepare the billing. There are other options and combinations of approaches in use, and the employer and the EAP vendor should determine which approach best meets their needs. Finally, a caution. Mistakes in bills and poor contract management are embarrassing and can leave the customer feeling that the EAP is not professional. Make sure your financial and billing systems are well managed and periodically reviewed.

Marketing Research

Marketing is expensive and marketing research can be valuable in making the best marketing decisions. EAP marketing research requires no unique methodologies — the research techniques used in any type of marketing can be used effectively with the EAP market. Some of the approaches we have found most helpful are outlined here, and sample research instruments are included in the Appendix.

1. *Customer Surveys:* Surveys of employees can be conducted before and after implementation of an EAP, after training, and after receiving counseling services. Periodic surveys of the people responsible for coordinating the EAP for the employer can help spot trouble points and emphasize strengths.
2. *Competition Studies:* Keep updated data on your competitors, their services, fees, strengths and weaknesses.
3. *Focus Groups and Individual Interviews:* Talk to your customers, write down what they say, and follow up. Customers can include employees, supervisors, clients, and referents. Share and discuss your findings with other staff.
4. *Marketing Evaluation:* You can develop simple record-keeping systems to document how people hear about you and the "conversion rate" for sales calls. This type of data is important in improving the effectiveness of marketing strategies.

The value of marketing research comes not from accumulating data, but from using the data in a systematic, planned manner. Involve as many staff members as possible in the research process from study design through data collection, to discussion of the results and action planning. Marketing research data will not give the final answer, but it can help narrow the uncertainties. Much of the information collected through evaluation and research studies can be analyzed from a marketing perspective and can be helpful in keeping current contracts and acquiring new business. Finally, if your EAP provides regular statistical reports to the company, have the marketing staff review these reports and how they are presented — statistical data should be seen as another service you provide and not just a report.

Marketing to Small Employers

Small companies make up 50 percent of the work force in the United States, and this group is clearly an underserved population when it comes to employee assistance. The cost of making a sales call is high, and

Marketing

many companies must be contracted to make it worthwhile to the EAP provider. Some ideas to make the job easier include

- Emphasize direct mail.
- Qualify your prospects through telemarketing.
- Work with organizations to develop a consortium (many companies are billed at the same time, given reports in aggregate, and trained together).

Types of prospects could include
- all stores in a shopping center
- all union machinists
- associations of lawyers/dentists
- small business association
- chamber of commerce
- employers associations

These small employers are accessible, and you know who makes the decisions. This type of client can offer security to the EAP provider. If you lose one, it will not be a significant financial loss, and you can build a base of business around small employers. (Also, see Perkins, 1986.)

Marketing the Internal Program

In this chapter, marketing has focused on how to promote and sell EAPs to organizations. The internal promotional effort is an ongoing process and should have a written plan. There are many ways to promote internally; some of these include

- supervisory training
- mailings to all employees at their homes as a reminder that this service is available
- newsletters
- presentations on the EAP in performance appraisal and other personnel training

Many internal EAPs have an in-house committee to help keep the program effective and visible. This committee should include people from as many different areas of the company as possible. In turn, these people can be individual public relations representatives in their respective departments.

Conclusions

There is no magic formula for marketing of employee assistance services. To be successful, each of many key elements must be addressed. Staying close to the customer is essential, but do not forget there are two customers: the client (employee) and the company who purchases these services. If the company's needs are not identified and met, there will be no clients to counsel. The "four p's" are all important, and direct sales will be a major emphasis for the EAP marketing plan. But perhaps the most important factor is a commitment from all staff members to work together to develop and deliver services that are needed and effective and to recognize that the end result of marketing is more help for more people.

Marketing

References

Bachrach, Ira N., "How to Choose and Use a Trademark," *Nation's Business*, March, 1983.

Burke, John D., *Advertising in the Marketplace*, New York, NY, McGraw-Hill Book Company, 1973.

Gaedeke, Ralph M., *Marketing in Private and Public Nonprofit Organizations*, Santa Monica, CA, Goodyear Publishing Company, Inc., 1977.

Goldman, R. L., et. al. "Marketing Employee Assistance Programs to Industry," *Health Marketing Quarterly*, 1(23) Winter 1983/Spring: 91-98, 1984.

Grantsmanship Center, "Program Planning and Proposal Writing," *Grantsmanship Center News*, 1978.

Kennedy, Eugene, *On Becoming a Counselor*, New York, NY, The Seabury Press, 1977.

Kinnear, Thomas C. and Kenneth L. Bernhardt, *Principles of Marketing*, Glenview, IL, Scott, Foresman and Company, 1983.

Kotler, P., *Marketing for Non-Profit Organizations*, New York, NY, Prentice Hall, 1982.

Marguiles, Walter P., "Make the Most of Your Corporate Identity," *Harvard Business Review*, July-August, 1977.

McMillan, Norman H., *Marketing Your Hospital: A Strategy for Survival*, Chicago, IL, American Hospital Publishing, Inc., 1981.

Peters, Thomas J., and Robert H. Waterman, Jr., *In Search of Excellence*, New York, NY, Harper Row Publishers, 1985.

Perkins, W.A. and D. L. Reynolds, "EAP Consortium Provides Vital Job Services to Small Employers," *Business and Health*, Jan/Feb: 52-53, 1986.

Reeves, Thomas and Judith G. Reeves, *Marketing Treatment Programs*, Jamul, CA, Reeves Communications, 1983.

Spicer, J. W., *Marketing*, Minneapolis, MN, University of Minnesota, School of Public Health, 1985.

Wilson, Larry, *Counselor Selling*, Bloomington, MN, Wilson Learning Corporation, 1978.

4
RESEARCH
Patricia Owen, Ph.D.

Patricia Owen is a licensed clinical psychologist with several years of experience in both the clinical and research areas of chemical dependency. She has written several articles for professional journals, including the Employee Assistance Quarterly. Currently she is the manager of Hazelden's Employee Assistance Services. Pat is a graduate of the University of Minnesota.

Introduction

Research on the characteristics and impact of employee assistance programs is improving. The basics of sound research are evident in many articles, and researchers are beginning to delineate the limitations of their studies. In spite of these advances, it is still common to find articles that freely cite anecdotes or loosely estimated dollar amounts of EAP savings. Unfortunately, this type of information is often only marginally accurate, and it conveys the false idea that sound EAP research has not been done. Several thorough critical

The EAP Solution

reviews of EAP research are available (Walker and Shain, 1983; Kurtz, Googins, and Howard, 1984; Spicer, Owen, and Levine, 1983), and the purpose here is not to repeat them. Instead, this chapter will acquaint the reader with some good examples of EAP research and suggest methods and topics that would continue to improve the field.

Current Research

When most people think of EAP research, they are likely to think of research that describes the users and outcomes of EAPs. Actually, there are numerous types of research that fall under the general heading of EAP research. Some of the main types are as follows:

1. *Supervisory training and involvement in EAP referrals.* Studies have been conducted to examine different methods of training supervisors, to detect troubled employees and make referrals, and to report on supervisors' perceptions and evaluations of the EAP process. Reports are also published on the effect of supervisory referral vs. self-referral on employees' outcomes.

2. *Characteristics of employees who use the EAP.* Studies of this type present information on the demographic and occupational characteristics of employees who use EAPs or who are considered to be troubled employees. Studies of EAP clients often provide information on the types of problems presented by the EAP client and/or assessed by the EAP counselor.

3. *Association between alcoholism and industrial accidents.* Numerous studies have been done to examine the relationship between alcohol use and accidents, particularly in the transportation fields.

4. *Association between chemical dependency and other health care costs.* Researchers using data from insurance companies and prepaid health plans have conducted and published numerous studies on the levels of health care utilization by identified alcoholics (and their families) before and after treatment for alcoholism.

5. *Outcomes of employees who use the EAP.* Studies in this area examine the existence of employees' problems before and after use of an EAP. Studies vary greatly in their use of comparison groups and the length of time the employees' behavior is examined.
6. *Effects of employee wellness programs.* These studies examine the relationship between health promotion activities in the workplace and evidence of improved lifestyle, behavior, or health.
7. *Cost analyses of EAP programs.* It is becoming increasingly important to examine the characteristics of a company's EAP in terms of its ability to save a company money, or at least to justify itself in terms of variables that can be associated with costs, such as employee turnover, absenteeism, and use of health care benefits. Researchers are becoming much more adept at designing sound research that includes cost analyses.

Each of these areas has a fairly good foundation of research. Two things, however, are apparent from this list. First, there are gaps between topics; and second, in spite of the gaps between some of the topics, the content of other topics actually overlaps. Figure 6 illustrates some of the gaps and overlapping areas in EAP research. Most EAP research pertains to Box 3, the referral process, and Box 4, the EAP program. For example, a report of this type might study the outcomes of clients referred to the EAP by their supervisors vs. those who went on their own accord.

To understand the gaps and overlapping areas, consider two hypothetical cases. The first, employee A, is an office manager in a company that has a clear policy prohibiting alcohol and other drug use during business hours and permits responsible use of alcohol at company events. The company climate is characterized by a participative style of decision making, progressiveness, and support. The company not only strongly endorses its EAP, but it has an active wellness program. For example, employee A quit smoking and received $500; now he routinely cashes in or converts his unused sick days into vacation days. He is a member of a softball

The EAP Solution

team sponsored by the company and swims daily at the YMCA, where he takes advantage of a health club discount provided by his company. When he uses a preferred provider suggested by his company's medical department, his copayments are significantly reduced. Employee A recognized he had an alcohol problem. He decided to go to the EAP at the suggestion of his family, after they read a brochure about the EAP program that came to their home. The EAP counselor referred him to a counseling clinic recommended as a preferred provider by his company's medical department, and he continued his recovery process by attending Alcoholics Anonymous. His supervisor and co-workers were supportive of his decision to receive help.

Figure 6
Components of EAP Research

1. Workplace	2. Company Programs	3. Referral Process
Company Policy	Employee Assistance Program	Supervisory vs. Self-referral
Company Culture	Wellness Program	Biomedical Screening
Employee Occupations	Health Insurance Incentives and Benefits	

4. EAP Program	5. Treatment	6. Follow-up/Aftercare
Referral vs. Counseling	Medical	Supervisory Involvement
Short-term vs. Ongoing Counseling	Psychiatric	Company Policy
Broadbrush or Alcohol-only	Chemical Dependency	Company Culture
In-house or Contractual	Inpatient	Ongoing Therapy
	Outpatient	Self-help Groups
	Self-help Groups	

In contrast, consider employee B. He is also an office manager, and his company contracts with the same EAP. However, his company has no stated policy on alcohol and other drug use, and it is common to meet for drinks at lunch. His company culture is characterized by centralized decision making, where rules and goals are set by the top executive officer. There is no company wellness program, and no incentive for using preferred providers for health-related problems. Employee B also had an alcohol problem and went to the EAP at the request of his family who received an informational brochure in the mail at home. He attended an outpatient counseling clinic and went to Alcoholics Anonymous. Employee B did not discuss his problem or decision to seek help with his supervisor or co-workers, who were apparently unaware of his problem.

Given the above set of circumstances, it is possible to imagine any of the following research studies:

- the relationship between company policy and employee alcoholism
- the relationship between company climate and employee alcoholism
- the relationship between wellness programs and employee alcoholism
- the relationship between health incentive programs and alcoholism treatment for employees
- the relationship between broadbrush EAPs and alcoholism treatment for employees
- evaluation of outpatient alcoholism treatment for employees

This list of research topics is just a sample of the pieces of the large picture (described by Figure 6) that an EAP researcher might be tempted to examine. Choosing one of these topics without considering the other mediating factors may give a distorted view of the relationship between work-related factors and alcohol use. In the example of employees A and B, it is clear that even though both of their companies use the same EAP, the mediating and causal factors in the development and resolution of their alcohol problems are likely to be very different. It is also important to keep in mind that other researchers not familiar with EAPs are going to examine other variables, perhaps including employee A and employee B in the same set of circumstances. For example, these researchers may examine the relationship between family dynamics and outcome of alcoholism treatment, without taking the work environment or the EAP into consideration.

A more concrete example is an extensive article on the relationship between employee lateness, absence, and turnover, in which twenty-four related articles are reviewed (Clegg, 1983), but alcoholism is not stressed. This is an excellent applied psychology article, just as many EAP research articles are excellent. However, it is unfortunate that the two fields seem to rarely consider variables that have importance for both of them. The main point of this section is to emphasize that while it is impossible for any single research project to measure all variables relative to a phenomenon, it is imperative to acknowledge the potential or unconsidered factors, and to relate the research findings with the larger general picture. In classic research theory, this is referred to as constructing a "nomological net" (Cronbach and Meehl, 1955).

Designing the EAP Research Study

Given the current state of the art of EAP research, certain factors need to be considered in designing future studies.

Ask the right questions. The most difficult and perhaps most important aspect of research design is problem identification. The first step at this stage is to state the hypothesis, and identify related, competing, or larger hypotheses. At this stage, it is important to gather information from experts in the field through discussion and review of related articles that have been published in journals or presented at conferences. The researcher should expect to revise or modify his or her hypothesis several times as new information is obtained. For example, an EAP researcher may initially construct a hypothesis relating employee absenteeism and alcohol problems. After reviewing the article mentioned earlier (Clegg, 1984), the researcher may want to relate the topic of job satisfaction to the hypotheses. It is common for a research project to be based on several hypotheses.

Choose appropriate variables. Basing a research project on carefully constructed hypotheses determines which variables to include in data collection. Too often, studies are done using the "shotgun" approach, where the researcher gathers all accessible or incidentally related data. Once a hypothesis is stated, the range of variables to consider is greatly reduced.

Two important matters regarding variable selection still remain. First, the researcher must decide how to measure the construct that is chosen. For example, "employee absenteeism" may be measured by retrospective self-report or by gathering information from company files. The concept of absenteeism may include tardiness and leaving work early, as well as missing full days. While no single method of objectifying an intangible construct such as absenteeism is correct, the researcher does best if the chosen variable is consistent with variables chosen by others doing similar research and if the variable is defined as specifically and objectively as possible. This will help ensure its measurement can be replicated by others.

Accessibility of data is the second important issue facing the researcher in choosing variables. Employers may be reluctant to allow access to data considered to be sensitive or confidential, such as employees' use of health benefits. Some of this reluctance can be overcome by slowly building trust through contacts between the company and the research team, as well as by devising creative ways to recode the data so numbers, rather than employee-identifying information, is actually in the hands of the researchers.

Data may also be difficult to access because of company reorganization. With the trend toward company mergers and takeovers, data that may once have been easy to access may become buried within a new bureaucracy, or simply discontinued. When this happens, the study may need to be modified or restarted, using other variables that are accessible. Several chapters in a recent government publication discuss problems of data collection at the work site and ways to anticipate or resolve them (Godwin, Lieberman, and Leukefeld, 1985).

Determine the sampling method and sample size. Many studies state subjects for the sample were "randomly selected." However, it appears likely that often the subjects in these studies were "haphazardly" selected. If random subject selection is to be done, it is best to state how the original population was defined and what exact method of random assignment or selection was used. For example, the original population may be all company supervisors. The sample from this population may be chosen through use of a random number table.

Size of the sample depends on two general factors: statistical power and representativeness. In the case of the former, the researcher must anticipate the type of statistical tests that will be used to analyze the data. Different types of analyses will have different sample size requirements. For example, multiple regression requires a larger sample than chi-square. A text by Cohen (1977) provides a guide to a statistical power analysis.

The second matter to consider is representativeness. EAP researchers often do epidemiological research. They may want to know the prevalence of alcohol and other drug problems among employees in a particular large company. Instead of surveying every employee, which can be difficult as well as costly, they can choose a sample from the work force whose responses will be reasonably representative of the total workplace. A text by Kish (1967) is one of the many excellent texts that describes methods for determining sample size and subject selection.

Choose a strong research design. Ideally, experimental designs would be used for EAP research. Troubled employees seeking help might be randomly assigned to see an EAP counselor, or are put on an EAP "waiting list," or some other form of nontreatment or alternative treatment. However, most pure experimental designs that are acceptable and ethical are difficult to create and implement. Variations on pure experimental designs are acceptable and can be quite impressive. A classic text about designing practical yet sophisticated research studies is *Quasi-Experimentation* by Cook and Campbell (1979).

Choose appropriate instruments. Questionnaires, surveys, interviews, and other tests or methods of measurement need to have adequate evidence of validity and reliability before they can be used appropriately in research. A typical example might be as follows: Imagine a researcher is examining the relationship between employee health and problems with alcohol and has decided to measure the concept of "health" by asking the employee a series of questions about the number of visits he or she has made to the doctor in the past six months. One indication of reliability is whether employees' responses are consistent or stable from one day to the next. If they were asked a relatively simple question, such as, "Did you see a physician in the past six months?" they probably would give the same responses at time one and time two. If the question was more complex, such as, "How many days were you ill during the past six months?" employees' responses may vary with their mood or the amount of time they were willing to admit. The former question would probably have a higher level of reliability than the latter.

An instrument cannot be valid unless it is reliable. A test is considered valid if it actually measures what it is intended to measure. The number of doctor visits may measure help-seeking as well as physical health; a retrospective report of number of days ill may also reflect preoccupation with health. A more valid measure of physical health may be a physician's report and laboratory results from an annual physical exam. This example highlights only a few of the important issues regarding reliability and validity. Reliability and validity can be measured statistically. Almost every statistics text reviews these basic concepts. For a thorough discussion, the reader is referred to Carmines and Zeller (1979).

How do the concepts of reliability and validity relate to the EAP researcher's choice of instruments? EAP researchers often need to measure concepts such as employees' attitudes or emotional status. Many times, a "homemade" self-report questionnaire is constructed and given to employees. For example, EAP clients may be asked to complete a ten-item questionnaire on stress. This questionnaire may have a great deal of face validity. Most people who look at it will agree that it seems to

The EAP Solution

be asking about stress. However, face validity has little bearing on actual validity or reliability. The researcher in this situation has two choices. The first is to review the literature and find a questionnaire that has already been developed and is satisfactory for the task at hand. This is an excellent course of action since the researcher benefits from using a test with known and acceptable levels of reliability and validity. This method of questionnaire standardization can take years of research and thousands of dollars. Another benefit from using an already-constructed instrument is that findings can be compared with previous and future research published by others. This is a benefit to the whole EAP field. An excellent source for finding standardized questionnaires is the *Mental Measurement Yearbook* (1978) or a text by Miller (1977).

The second option is to create a new instrument. As already mentioned, this is an extremely complex and time-consuming process. Hundreds of completed questionnaires must be gathered from many different samples, and the data obtained must be subjected to repeated statistical analysis to test for reliability and validity. Most EAP researchers do not have the luxury of spending years of work on a project that will have only long-term, rather than immediate benefits. An excellent text on instrument development is by Nunnally (1967).

Choose the appropriate statistical analysis. Long before the data are collected, the researcher should know which statistical analyses are appropriate for the study. Two common problems are evident in many EAP studies. Often, no statistical tests are used and yet columns of univariate percentages are examined for what appear to be significant differences. The larger the number of percentages computed and compared, the larger the chance of finding a spurious difference between groups. The second problem is at the opposite extreme; multivariate statistical tests are used in an attempt to account for the wide range of variables. However, a small sample is used, and the analysis is not repeated on a different sample. Because multivariate analyses capitalize on chance variations within a sample, large samples with replications are needed before conclusions can be drawn. Besides basic statistical texts, two other sources are helpful to the researcher in choosing appropriate statistical tests: one is a statistical guide published by the Institute for Social Research at the University of Michigan (1981), and the other is a pair of research books by Marks (1982 a,b).

Disseminate the results. All too often, huge quantitites of data are amassed, yet the final step of reporting results is done only informally in in-house meetings or at conferences and is never written, distributed, or published. This is commonly known as the file-drawer problem. It is very important for the EAP researcher to provide a presentation and interpretation of the results that is understandable and enlightening to both the general audience and the technical or professional readers. Two sources offer suggestions for accomplishing this and help the researcher anticipate problems (Friedman, 1985; and Deshpande and Zaltman, 1982).

Cost-Analysis Methods

In today's competitive business and health care climate, questions of economic benefit often arise. While statistical significance and clinical significance are of critical importance for the EAP researcher, decision makers within a company may be most interested in financial significance. All of the research principles discussed here can be translated and used to conduct a cost-analysis study. As with every type of research, the critical factor is the soundness of the methodology, more than the actual content of inquiry.

Cost-analysis studies are becoming prevalent in EAP research and in related areas. The basic question is, "Does our EAP save the company money?" This is an important question, and one that usually has many components. While it is impossible to introduce all of the aspects of cost-analysis studies in this chapter, a brief review of concepts followed by some methodological reminders are given here. For a more thorough review, the reader is referred to a monograph by Spicer and Owen (1985), and a book by Warner and Luce (1982).

The EAP Solution

Figure 7
Cost-Analysis Terms

Cost-Containment Activities: Strategies used to reduce expenditures or control rising costs. Typically do not focus on long-term issues.

>   Examples: Prepaid systems, claims review, use of preferred providers, increasing deductibles.

Cost-Impact/Offset Studies: Determination of areas where cost savings occur as a result of providing a service. Does not compare models nor is a dollar estimate of the savings required.

>   Examples: Showing the percentage reduction in absenteeism following referral by the EAP.

Cost-Effectiveness Studies: Calculation of the cost of obtaining some desired *outcome*. Will typically be a ratio of the cost of obtaining a result divided by the number of desired outcomes (not necessarily expressed in dollars). Can compare different ways of achieving the same objective.

>   Examples: Comparing inpatient and outpatient programs by dividing the real costs of each by the number of improved clients.

Cost-Benefit Analysis: Comparison of the benefits of a program with its costs. Requires consideration of all long-term and related benefits and costs. Can be used to compare very different programs.

>   Examples: A comparison of an employee hypertension screening program with an alcoholism treatment program.

The New Concepts

There are many groups now involved in examining the issues of health care costs and proposing solutions to the problems. Unfortunately, these groups are not all in agreement in terms of the goals and activities necessary to accomplish cost control (see Figure 7).

One of the most commonly used words is cost containment. Cost containment includes strategies used to control the short-term costs of providing chemical dependency or mental health services. Some of these strategies include utilization review, prepaid services, mandated length of stay, use of outpatient as opposed to inpatient care, and case management (see Figure 8). Most discussions of cost containment are focused on the cost of treatment or services with little reference to long-term outcome or quality of care. Cost containment is a response to providing services with limited resources. The rationale for cost containment is that there is a limited amount of funding and therefore all costs must be tightly controlled in order to maintain control of health care expenditures. Unfortunately, there may be an assumption that health care providers overcharge for services and are not efficient in the use of their resources. Therefore, cost containment often operates on the premise that there is waste in the system, and by mandating maximum amounts of funding to be spent, costs can be controlled. Cost-containment research typically measures health care expenditures before and after a new cost-management program is implemented, which may include the employee assistance program.

A second concept often used is cost impact or cost offset. Most previous research has been cost-offset research. In a cost-offset/impact study, the objective is to demonstrate that the costs of providing employee assistance services are offset by reductions in health care costs and other areas following services. Cost offset is not the same as cost containment. Where cost containment starts with the premise of controlling expenditures, cost-offset programs seek to demonstrate that there is an economic return when employee assistance services are available because of reductions in illness, unemployment, legal problems, etc. However, if an employer has a limited amount of money and is concerned about not exceeding that amount, the employer may not spend more because of the cost impact of the service. It is just as important that many of the savings resulting from employee assistance programs will not directly accrue to the employer. The offsets may be in areas outside of the employer's concern. Examples of these would be legal problems, productivity, and employee morale — areas that are not directly and easily convertible into dollars on a balance sheet.

The EAP Solution

Figure 8
Common Cost-Containment Strategies

Using less-expensive services

    Negotiating discounts (PPOs)
    Prepaid systems (HMOs, IPAs)

Using less-expensive treatment options

    Using programs with shorter length of stay
    Using outpatient/ambulatory care rather than inpatient/acute care

Using cost-control methods

    Second opinion services; claims review ("usual and customary services")
    Reviewing length of stay; admission certification
    Payment by diagnostic group
    Limiting services to certain groups (such as readmissions)

Reducing the corporation's contribution

    Changing deductible/copayment policies; decreasing coverage
    Developing new policies; consumer incentives

Cost-effectiveness analysis is a more sophisticated type of research that compares the cost of achieving an outcome by different service models. "CEA permits comparison of cost per unit of effectiveness against competing alternatives designed to serve the same basic purpose" (Warner and Luce, 1982: 48). The results are usually expressed as a ratio of the cost of obtaining a result divided by the number of desired outcomes. In cost-effectiveness analysis, the service cost may be expressed in dollars but the outcome measure can be expressed behaviorally, as through absenteeism or abstinence rates. However, cost-effectiveness analysis does not permit comparison of programs with different objectives, nor does it measure the inherent worth of a program. CEA tells you: for every dollar of input in a program, x units of outcome are achieved. An example of cost-effectiveness analysis is in Figure 9. It shows two employee assistance programs — Company A and Company B. Both programs are similar in model and employee populations with the same utilization rates, and for our purposes, serving the same number of eligible employees. Although Company A is a less expensive program, averaging $10 per employee compared to Company B's $16 per employee, no assumptions can be made about cost effectiveness by only knowing the total cost of the program. However, if there is a measure of program effectiveness, such as reduction in absenteeism, a comparison of the total cost of the program against the reduction in absenteeism will indicate which program is more cost effective. In this example, Program B is more cost effective. In Program B it costs approximately $400 to achieve one unit of reduced absenteeism where in Company A it costs $500 per unit of reduced absenteeism. The importance of this example is to demonstrate that total or per unit costs have no necessary relationship to cost effectiveness. Cost effectiveness must be predicated on the measurement of some outcome against the cost of obtaining that outcome. Cost effectiveness is not synonymous with cost containment, nor with cost benefit, nor with cost-impact/offset studies. However, for many funders and corporations the issue may not be cost effectiveness, but rather containing the total dollar outlay for health care. If funds are strained, the employer may choose the least expensive provider even if another provider might be more cost effective. The provider should understand the logic and rationale of the decision maker and recognize the decision maker will not always have the ability or resources to select the most cost-effective program.

The EAP Solution

Figure 9
Cost-Effectiveness Example

Company	Cost/Employee	Annual Cost	Utilization Rate	Reduction in Absenteeism	Cost-Effectiveness Ratio
A (100 employees)	$10	$1000	5%/yr	2 days/yr	$1000/2 = $500
B (100 employees)	$16	$1600	5%/yr	4 days/yr	$1600/4 = $400

Interpretation: Although Company A has the least-costly program on a per employee and total cost basis, Company B achieves a positive outcome (reduction in absenteeism) at a lower cost. Company B therefore has a more cost-effective program.

Cost-benefit analysis is the most sophisticated type of economic analysis where all costs before service, the service cost itself, and the outcomes or benefits are expressed in dollars (Levin, 1983: 21). The end result, or net benefit, is a monetary measure of the program's benefits minus costs. Because CBA results in a standardized monetary measure, very different programs can be compared (for example, a hypertension screening program with an employee assistance program). However, because health services have results, such as abstinence, that are very difficult to express monetarily, there have been only partial attempts at CBA in the health care field. The reader should be cautious in accepting many studies reported to be cost-benefit studies, as they are likely to be cost-offset studies.

Some Reminders About Cost Analysis

Include all variables that affect cost. Most EAP cost-analysis studies examine the costs of troubled employees for a company before and after referral or treatment or both. While this has merits and can help determine the effectiveness of the EAP, there are other factors to consider. The cost of the EAP and the cost of the treatment should be weighed with the cost of producing the desired outcome. If ongoing research is conducted to monitor the costs and savings associated with the EAP program, then, in all fairness, the cost of the research should also be entered into the equation.

Research

If it is necessary to assign monetary values to the variables, the values must be clear and realistic. EAP cost analysis should recognize the greatest impact of the EAP may be in areas difficult to express monetarily, as shown in Figure 10. For most studies, a simple description of the changes in costly behaviors (e.g., absenteeism, use of health benefits, turnover), speaks well enough for itself without attaching dollar signs to the variables. A disadvantage of dollar amounts is they lose their meaning or significance rather quickly. An advantage of using dollar amounts to quantify behavior is that monetary values attract attention. The finding that use of an EAP is associated with a drop in absenteeism of x percent may not be as compelling as the related finding that use of an EAP is associated with a savings of x amount of dollars. However, it may be more accurate, since it is probably impossible to attach consistently correct dollar amounts to employee behavior.

Figure 10
Measuring the Cost-Impact of an EAP

Benefits That Can Be Easily Measured In Dollars

Health benefits utilization, medical claims
Accidents, injuries
Worker's compensation, unemployment insurance
Sick leave, disability

Benefits That Are More Difficult To Measure In Dollars

Absenteeism, absences
Turnover, terminations

Benefits That Are Very Difficult To Measure in Dollars

Morale
Job performance
Quality of employee life and work environment
Long-term health improvement

The EAP Solution

Future Directions in EAP Research

As the quality and diversity of EAP research increases, several changes are likely to occur.

1. There will be research on which *EAP components* are most effective, rather than continued research on whether EAPs, in general, are effective. This type of study requires a great deal of work to first define EAP components, and to describe how they interrelate to each other and to other organizational programs, such as health benefit packages and wellness programs.
2. There will be more research on which employees benefit most (and in what ways) from EAP services. Current research already indicates that employees vary to the extent they use insurance benefits and sick time. It is generally true that a relatively small proportion of employees account for a relatively large proportion of absenteeism and use of health insurance. Analagous to this, it may be a particular subgroup of employees is most likely to benefit from intervention.
3. Research will stem from large data bases and from management information systems that will allow relocations and enhancement of original studies. As more researchers realize the costs and time involved of doing good EAP research, cooperation in the form of sharing data and expertise will become more necessary and desirable. Computers will make ongoing data collection and storage routine and will allow the researcher to take advantage of large data bases.

In summary, EAP research is coming of age, and the field is rapidly becoming more sophisticated in research design and analysis. As this occurs, EAP researchers are accumulating the benefits and problems that face researchers in general.

References

Andrews, F. A., L. Klem, T. N. Davidson, P. M. O'Malley, and W. L. Rodgers, *A Guide for Selecting Statistical Techniques for Analyzing Social Science Data*, Ann Arbor, MI, Institute for Social Research, 1981.

Buros, O. K. (ed.), *The Eighth Mental Measurements Yearbook*, Highland Park, NJ, Gryphon Press, 1976.

Carmines, E. G., and R. A. Zeller, *Reliability and Validity Assessment*, Beverly Hills, CA, Sage Publications, 1979.

Clegg, C. W., "Psychology of Employee Lateness, Absence, and Turnover: A Methodological Critique and an Empirical Study," *Journal of Applied Psychology*, 68, 88-101, 1983.

Cohen, J., *Statistical Power for the Behavioral Sciences*, New York, NY, Academic Press, 1977.

Cook, T. D. and D. T. Campbell, *Quasi-Experimentation: Design and Analysis Issues for Field Settings*, Boston, MA, Houghton-Mifflin, 1979.

Cronbach, L. J., and P. E. Meehl, "Construct Validity in Psychological Tests," *Psychological Bulletin*, 52, 281-302, 1955.

Deshpande, R. and G. Zaltman, "Factors Affecting the Use of Market Research Information: A Path Analysis," *Journal of Marketing Research*, 19: 14-26, 1982.

Friedman, D. E., "Research Utilization by the Business Community," in D. F. Godwin, M. L. Lieberman, and C. G. Leukefeld (eds.), *The Business of Doing Worksite Research*, Rockville, MD, Alcohol, Drug Abuse, and Mental Health Administration, 1985.

Godwin, D. F., M. L. Lieberman, and C. G. Leukefeld, *The Business of Doing Worksite Research*, Rockville, MD, Alcohol, Drug Abuse, and Mental Health Administration, 1985.

Kish, L., *Survey Sampling*, New York, Wileg, 1967.

Kurtz, N. R., B. Googins, and W. C. Howard, "Measuring the Success of Occupational Alcoholism Programs," *Journal of Studies on Alcohol*, 45, 33-45, 1984.

Levin, H. M., *Cost-Effectiveness: A Primer*, Beverly Hills, CA, Sage Publications, 1983.

Marks, R. G., *Designing a Research Project*, London, England, Lifetime Learning, 1982a.

Marks, R. G., *Analyzing Research Data*, London, England, Lifetime Learning, 1982b.

Miller, D. C., *Handbook of Research Design and Social Measurement*, New York, NY, Longman, 1977.

Nunnally, J. C., *Psychometric Theory*, New York, NY, McGraw-Hill, 1967.

Roman, P. M., "Substance Abuse and the Workplace: Dimensions of Extent and Needed Knowledge," In D. F. Godwin, et al. (Eds.) *The Business of Doing Worksite Research*, Rockville, MD, Alcohol, Drug Abuse, and Mental Health Adminstration, 1985.

Rossi, P. H., "Problems in the Utilization of Applied Social Research," In D. F. Godwin, M. L. Lieberman, and C. G. Leukefeld (eds.), *The Business of Doing Worksite Research*, Rockville, MD, Alcohol, Drug Abuse, and Mental Health Administration.

Spicer, J., P. Owen, and D. Levine, *Evaluating Employee Assistance Programs*, Center City, MN, Hazelden Educational Materials, 1984, order number 1931.

Spicer, J., and P. Owen, *Finding the Bottom Line*, Center City, MN, Hazelden Research Reports, 1985.

Trice, H. M., "Studying Troubled Employees: Gaining and Keeping Research Access," In D. F. Godwin et al., *The Business of Doing Worksite Research*, Rockville, MD, Alcohol, Drug Abuse, and Mental Health Administration, 1985.

Walker, K., and M. Shain, "Employee Assistance Programming: In Search of Effective Interventions for the Problem-Drinking Employee," *British Journal of Addiction, 78,* 291-303, 1983.

Warner, K. E., and B. R. Luce, *Cost-Benefit and Cost Effectiveness Analysis in Health Care: Principles, Practice and Potential,* Ann Arbor, MI, Health Administration Press, 1982.

5
EVALUATION
Donald Jones, M.A.

Donald Jones is the Manager of Consultation Services for Hazelden. He has extensive experience in EAP evaluation, having developed the information system (SCORE) used by Hazelden and also by other EAPs using this service. Don has written several reports and articles on EAP evaluation and regularly teaches in Hazelden's EAP workshop. His master's degree in Human Development is from St. Mary's College, Winona, Minnesota.

Reasons for Conducting Evaluation

As the employee assistance field matures, more programs are conducting program evaluation activities. Program managers are doing a better job of monitoring and evaluating their services.

The interest in EAP evaluation is growing for a number of reasons. Programs are becoming more formally established and operated. Many EAPs began on an informal basis, with one recovering employee attempting to identify and help co-workers with drinking

The EAP Solution

problems. Now, many of these EAPs have become institutionalized, with written policies, set hours and services, standardized record keeping, and formalized training and communications. In this environment, systematic data collection and reporting are quickly replacing the type of anecdotal, case history approach used in the past.

As EAPs have matured, they have also become more complex. The broadbrush model, in particular, is a complicated set of services designed to handle all types of personal problems and to serve family members as well as employees. A full service program may also provide twenty-four-hour accessibility, crisis counseling, employee and supervisory training, management consultation, and health promotion activities. Clearly, program administration has become more complex, and more systematic information is needed to monitor and manage program services.

It is obvious that the employee assistance field has also become more competitive. External providers compete with in-house programs for corporate contracts, and a diverse group of new providers is entering the fray. Hospitals, mental health centers, treatment programs, and private therapists are now selling EAP services. In order to compete, more programs are collecting data to document their performance and demonstrate their effectiveness to potential customers.

Skyrocketing corporate health care costs — and the pressures for cost containment — have changed the EAP environment. Because EAPs systematically refer employees and family members to covered services, corporations are very interested in both the cost and the quality of the services provided. Whatever the EAP is doing to control health care costs, more data are invariably needed on the numbers of referred employees, the costs of the providers used, and the units of service delivered.

In addition to containing costs, many corporations expect their employee assistance programs to effect cost savings by reducing health care utilization and improving work attendance and job performance for EAP clients. This type of cost-impact evaluation requires extensive company data and involves sophisticated statistical analysis.

Barriers to Program Evaluation

Despite the increased interest in EAP evaluation and research, several barriers still exist. Employee assistance is a relatively new field and lacks a history of scientific investigation. Even contemporary program managers often lack the formal training needed to conduct program evaluation.

Another barrier is the diversity of the field itself. There are three primary models: occupational alcoholism, broadbrush, and wellness models which are offered by both internal and external programs. This diversity makes it difficult to generalize from the findings on any one program and to develop standardized evaluation tools and techniques across program types.

Another disincentive for EAP evaluation has been the absence of reporting requirements for program licensure or accreditation. If the host company does not require much reporting, then EAPs are under no other obligation to evaluate themselves. In this respect, employee assistance is somewhat behind the field of alcohol or other drug treatment, which has responded to numerous funding, regulatory, and accreditation bodies.

There are also a number of practical limitations to EAP evaluation. Of primary importance is the concern for client confidentiality which is the cornerstone of any job-based program. While recent advances in client numbering and computer coding techniques have facilitated data gathering, client confidentiality must still be safeguarded. In the area of cost-impact evaluation, the accuracy and accessibility of employer records are also limiting factors. Finally, there is the high financial cost — the costs associated with defining, collecting, storing, retrieving, analyzing, and reporting program evaluation data.

Recommendations for Evaluation

Given these barriers and limitations on evaluating their programs, where should EAP managers focus their attention? Before beginning an evaluation study,

The EAP Solution

two questions can be asked to help define the focus of the research. The first question is: *What is the major goal of the EAP*? The answer to this question will depend on the type of EAP model, as shown below.

EAP Model	Primary Corporate Goal
Alcohol or other drug	Recovery of addicted employees
Broadbrush	Successful referral of troubled employees
Wellness/health promotion	Improved health of employees
Marketing strategy	Increased business for the provider
Cost containment	Reduction in health care costs

An employee assistance program cannot be all things to all people, and the emphasis in the evaluation should be on those goals that are congruent with the model. The best current example of this is the emphasis on cost containment. Because cost containment is typically a short-term objective, the health promotion model can make claims of having a more long-term positive cost benefit, but may find it very difficult to show immediate savings.

Once the reasonableness of the overall goal has been determined, the second question is: *Who is the audience*? No single evaluation study can address everyone's concerns, and the evaluator should spend time in the early stages listing and prioritizing possible questions (and testing the soundness of these questions against the overall model and goal). Examples of some typical questions are

Group	Possible Evaluation Questions:
Top management	Is the program cost effective? Does it increase our productivity? What proportion of our employees is using the program? What main problem areas are common in our organization? Does the EAP help prevent accidents, absenteeism?

Evaluation

Employee using EAP	Are the services helpful? Are clients treated with respect and courtesy? Are my contacts with the EAP kept confidential? Is the location convenient and appropriate?
Supervisors	Are the EAP services available when I need them? Does an employee's job performance improve after using the EAP? Will the EAP make my job easier?
The EAP administrator or counselor	What types of problems do employees bring to us? Are we making helpful and appropriate assessments and referrals? Are we effective in helping employees maintain or improve their work performance? Are employees satisfied with our service?
Unions	Does the EAP provide an alternative to dismissing an employee? How will this program affect grievance and arbitration procedures? Is there a penalty for the employees using the EAP?

(Adapted from discussions by Schramm et al., 1978)

The next step is to view these questions from an evaluation perspective. Two types of evaluation activities — process and outcome — can be conducted. *Process evaluation looks at how the program is functioning.* In the employee assistance field, process evaluation can answer these types of questions:

- What is the program utilization rate?
- Who, in general terms, is using the EAP?
- How effectively is the EAP penetrating the host organization?
- How do clients arrive at the EAP?

The EAP Solution

- What are the assessed client problems?
- Where are EAP clients referred?

These process questions are answered by ongoing program monitoring and reporting systems. The basic question is: Is the program operating as planned?

Outcome evaluation examines the effects or outcomes of a program. The basic question is: Is the program effective? The primary focus is typically on the EAP client, and the following questions could be addressed:

- Does the client contact the EAP referral?
- Is the client satisfied with the EAP referral?
- Do the client's problems improve?
- Is the client satisfied, overall, with EAP services?

If possible, outcome evaluation should also look at benefits to the company. Of course, the company can experience a number of real, but intangible, benefits such as improved employee morale. Most companies, however, seem interested in the economic benefits resulting from the EAP, specifically

- Is the EAP helping to contain corporate health care costs?
- Is the EAP producing any cost savings to the corporation, in the areas of employee health care utilization, work attendance, and job performance?

Overview

All of the previously listed processes and outcome evaluation questions will be addressed here. Process evaluation data are presented and compared for three different EAP models: two internal broadbrush programs and an external broadbrush program (Hazelden Employee Assistance). Because information is provided by the same data collection system, side-by-side program comparisons are possible. And the large size of the three data bases gives us more confidence in the findings. However, this chapter is not intended as a summary of EAP research. For a review of the literature and discussion of research design, consult *Evaluating Employee Assistance Programs: A Sourcebook for the Administrator and Counselor* (Spicer, Owen, and Levine, 1983). And for a more comprehensive treatment of cost-impact analysis, refer to *Finding the Bottom Line: The Cost Impact of Employee Assistance and Chemical Dependency Treatment Programs* (Spicer and Owen, 1985). Both books are published by Hazelden Research.

Services Evaluation

The program monitoring data presented here are produced by the Hazelden computerized EAP monitoring system, SCORE. The data describe 1984-85 program utilization for three very large employee assistance programs in the United States. The three programs are all formal, broadbrush, multisite EAPs which provide assessment/referral counseling for employees and their dependents. All three have written policies and formalized training and communication packages. The two internal programs have a long history within their companies. The external program (Hazelden) has been serving the companies for an average of three years.

All three EAPs are based on the same comprehensive or broadbrush approach. In this type of program, employees and families can receive help for all types of problems, not only for alcohol or other drug abuse. Although they share this common philosophy, the three programs are different.

The first — Hazelden Employee Assistance Services — is an externally provided service. It is staffed by Hazelden Employee Assistance counselors, rather than by company employees. Hazelden data includes information from thirty small- and mid-size companies served by a home office staff in Minnesota. The majority of these companies are high technology and service industries with predominantly white-collar employees.

The other two EAPs are similar in that both are internal broadbrush programs staffed by company employees. One of these companies is a high technology manufacturing company in the health care industry. The third EAP serves a large transportation company. This last EAP has the longest history and a strong emphasis on chemical dependency problems.

Other EAP monitoring data are certainly available. The significance of these findings is that the information is collected and reported in the same way.

The EAP Solution

Therefore, the differences among the three data bases are due to the characteristics of the three programs and the companies they serve and are not an artifact of the evaluation methods themselves. However, before looking at the data we must take a brief look at the data collection system and the methods used to count EAP clients and calculate program utilization rates.

Program Utilization: A Definition

Surprisingly, there is not a consistent method for arriving at the most basic measure of program operation — the utilization rate. Therefore, it is important to explain how the utilization rates presented here are calculated. There are three elements in the equation: the number of EAP clients, the number of eligible employees, and a defined time period.

How are EAP clients defined? The Hazelden monitoring system counts *any* person who goes through the assessment/referral process with an employee assistance counselor. This includes family members, referring supervisors (whose problem is a troubled employee), returning clients (who are reassessed), and telephone counseling cases.

While all of these people are counted as clients and described in utilization reports, the utilization rate is based on a more conservative number — the number of *employee families* who contact the EAP. (This approach is used because many employers pay for EAP services based on the number of employee families who are eligible to use the program.) The number of EAP client families is not affected if several members of the same family contact the EAP, or if the same people recontact the program.

The other two parts of the utilization formula are easier to define. The number of eligible employees is the number who are covered by the EAP. For reporting purposes, the time period is a year. (This is because many EAPs are funded on an annual basis.) Thus, *the utilization rate is the number of employee families who use the EAP during a year, divided by the number of eligible employees.* A sample calculation is shown in Table 1.

Evaluation

Table 1
Sample Calculation of Annual Utilization Rate

A. Number of EAP clients	240
B. Number of EAP employee families	200
C. Number of eligible employee families	2,000
D. Annual program utilization rate (B/C)	10%

Program Utilization: A Comparison

What is the program utilization rate? Now that the formula has been defined, the utilization rates for the three EAPs can be compared. As Table 2 shows, the transportation company has the lowest annual utilization at 3.2 percent. However, it should be pointed out that current utilization has increased significantly because of referrals to the EAP resulting from the company's urinalysis screening program and referrals for problems other than alcohol and other drugs.

The external broadbrush program has a higher utilization at 5.3 percent. The internal broadbrush achieves the highest utilization at 8.0 percent. This could be due to its broader scope and its internal location with the company. As will be shown later, both internal programs have much higher rates of supervisory referrals than the external program.

Differences in utilization can be due to a number of factors other than the program model itself. EAP training, communications, accessibility, and staffing all affect utilization. For instance, Hazelden has found the number of new EAP clients increases dramatically immediately after employee training sessions or mailings to employee homes. Nevertheless, the differences in utilization rates among the three EAPs are significant and should be kept in mind as the other data are reviewed.

The EAP Solution

Table 2
Annual Program Utilization Rate

Type of Industry	Mixed	High Tech Manufacturing	Transportation
Number of Eligible Employees	33,362	28,469	41,198
Number of EAP Clients	2,288	2,597	1,673
Number of EAP Client Families	1,765	2,265	1,288
Annual Utilization Rate (# Families/# Employees)	5.3%	8.0%	3.2%

Client Characteristics

Who, in general terms, is using the EAP? This is an important process evaluation question. An employee assistance program is intended to serve any and all employees (and their dependents) who are experiencing personal problems. Therefore, one would anticipate a diverse client population, rather than a typical EAP client profile.

The proportion of family members in the EAP caseload is a key variable because problems in an employee's family can affect a person's job performance. Conversely, the employee's problems can certainly affect the spouse and children, therefore the entire family may need help. For both of these reasons, the level of family participation deserves close attention.

All three programs are successful in recruiting family members (Table 3). Surprisingly, the transportation company has the highest percentage of dependents (26%), even though it does not focus on marital or family relationship problems. All three programs have the same ratio of 1.3 clients per family. This means that, on the average, about one in every three families has more than one client.

Evaluation

In terms of *client gender*, the first two programs both serve more females (approximately 60%) than males. The preponderance of males in the transportation company explains why the majority of its clients (74%) are males.

For all programs, *client age* ranges from less than 20 to more than 60, with an average of 33 to 35 years. Although two-thirds of all clients are between the ages of 20 and 40 years, the programs are serving clients of all age groups. Similarly, *client marital status* is diverse.

Table 3
Client Characteristics

	External Broadbrush Programs (N = 2,288)	Manufacturing Company (N = 2,597)	Transportation Company (N = 1,673)
Status			
Employee	80%	86%	74%
Family member	20%	14%	26%
Gender			
Male	38%	41%	74%
Female	62%	59%	26%
Age			
Less than 20 years	7%	4%	6%
20 to 29 years	34%	27%	26%
30 to 39 years	36%	38%	41%
40 to 49 years	15%	20%	16%
50 to 59 years	7%	9%	9%
60 years or more	1%	2%	2%
Average age	33 years	35 years	34 years
Marital Status			
Married	56%	58%	60%
Single	27%	19%	18%
Divorced/separated	16%	20%	20%
Other	1%	3%	2%

The EAP Solution

Program Penetration

How effectively is the EAP penetrating the company? The term *penetration* is often confused with utilization. Actually, *penetration is utilization by a specific group.* Program penetration can refer to many types of groups — the estimated number of troubled employees, family members, female employees, etc. Penetration into a company's work force is probably the most useful concept. Generally, the EAP client population should be representative of the entire company work force. To assess penetration, two measures should be taken: vertical (by employee occupation and seniority) and horizontal (by division or location).

Table 4 shows program penetration data for the three EAP models. The first two programs serve employees in all occupational levels from top management to unskilled labor. The occupational categories for the transportation company are unique to that industry and are not shown here. However, data indicate that the chemical dependency-focused EAP also penetrates all of its company's occupational groups.

The programs are also serving employees with varying levels of seniority, ranging from less than one to more than twenty years. Average seniority is seven years for the two programs and twelve years for the third program. These high averages have cost-impact implications. By helping long-term, valued employees, the EAPs are probably saving money by lowering employee turnover of key staff.

The two internal programs also have good horizontal penetration into their companies. The transportation company achieves utilization rates between three percent and five percent in ten of its twelve regions. The manufacturing company has rates between five percent and ten percent in 19 of 22 locations.

Together, these data indicate that the EAPs are effective in penetrating their respective companies. In other words, there are no apparent gaps in service delivery. Where possible, these types of EAP client data should be compared with similar data on all employees to make sure that the EAP caseload is truly representative of the company's work force.

Evaluation

Table 4
Employee Occupational Data

	External Broadbrush Programs (N = 1,765)	Manufacturing Company (N = 2,265)	Transportation Company (N = 1,288)
Occupational Group			
Administrative/managerial	23%	17%	—
Professional	6%	4%	—
Technical	20%	16%	—
Sales	7%	5%	—
Skilled craft	11%	21%	—
Clerical	26%	20%	—
Unskilled labor	6%	17%	—
Length of Service			
One year or less	11%	11%	1%
2 to 5 years	42%	36%	33%
6 to 10 years	29%	25%	28%
11 to 15 years	11%	15%	18%
16 to 20 years	6%	8%	8%
More than 20 years	2%	6%	12%
Average length of service	7 years	7 years	12 years

Referral Sources

How clients arrive at the EAP is an important operational question for a number of reasons. First, the EAP should have a broad base of support — from employees, supervisors, and family members at the least. The number of referrals from each of these groups is one indication of support. Referral data are also a measure of program implementation. If EAP trainings and policies are effective, supervisors will refer troubled employees. If program communications are effective, family members will also make referrals.

The EAP Solution

Referral data for the three EAP models are shown in Table 5. The transportation company program has the highest rate of referrals from supervisors (24%). This is not surprising because supporting supervisors in their role is a high priority for EAP staff. The program's internal location also facilitates supervisory referrals. Organizationally, supervisors probably find it easier to make referrals to a program within the company. The focus on alcohol or other drug problems may also be a factor. Compared with other troubled employees, a chemically dependent employee's performance will be more visibly impaired and more likely to lead to a supervisory referral. By serving a transportation industry, this EAP also covers public safety issues requiring supervisory action with troubled employees.

Supervisory referrals for the manufacturing company are slightly lower at twenty percent. The external broadbrush is the lowest at six percent despite training of company supervisors. This lower rate could be explained by the program's external location and less supervisory training, which might make supervisors less likely to refer. Also, as indicated in Table 4, the external program serves more white-collar employees, and deteriorating job performance is harder to detect in this group than among blue-collar groups. However, if supervisors are not referring employees whose performance is impaired by personal problems, the external broadbrush model is not fully operational.

The external program has the highest rate of self-referrals (70%). In this respect, it functions more as an early intervention/prevention program — presumably before problems become serious enough to affect work performance. Research on employee referrals to Hazelden treatment (Spicer, 1979) has found earlier intervention does occur. Compared to a matched sample of other patients, employer referrals were younger (42 vs. 49 years) and had shorter histories of problem drinking (6.8 vs. 8.9 years). These findings are important because it is generally assumed that early treatment for chemical dependency leads to better outcomes. Also, the employer benefits from earlier intervention into the job performance decline associated with alcoholism.

Evaluation

Table 5
Referral Sources

	External Broadbrush Programs (N = 2,288)	Manufacturing Company (N = 2,597)	Transportation Company (N = 1,673)
Self	70%	54%	42%
Family Member	10%	13%	19%
Supervisor (Formal)	2%	8%	15%
Supervisor (Informal)	4%	12%	9%
Other Employee	2%	5%	5%
Other	12%	8%	10%

Problem Assessment

The assessed client problems are a key measure of program functioning for any EAP model and a controversial subject in the field. The question is complicated by a number of issues. The first issue is the problem in estimating the number of impaired employees in the work force. These estimates are often assumed to be valid for all companies. However, there is reason to believe the prevalence of alcoholism varies across industries and occupations. And even less is known about the prevalence of marital, familial, emotional, financial, or legal problems in the work force.

The EAP Solution

The second issue is a methodological one. How are the problems assessed by EAP counselors? If an employee with a drinking problem does contact the EAP, the next question is whether he or she is correctly assessed. Research on the Hazelden EAP has found shifts occur between the types of problems presented by clients and those assessed by counselors. Overall, counselors assess more emotional, alcohol or other drug, and physical/sexual abuse problems than clients present. Conversely, staff assess fewer occupational, financial, educational, and job stress problems than are presented by clients. As expected, the largest discrepancy occurs in the area of alcohol or other drug problem assessment, where more than half (56%) of the clients present a different problem. Interestingly, this level of discrepancy is lower for the alcohol program, where 27 percent of the clients assessed with an alcohol or other drug problem initially presented something different.

Obviously, reporting the number of employees who present alcohol or other drug problems is not a reliable diagnostic measure. Even the counselor's assessment of alcoholism is problematic due to the general lack of standardized diagnostic tools in employee assistance (and in alcoholism treatment generally). EAP client problem assessment is not a simple subject. The assessment process used by EAP staff should be described whenever problem data are presented.

Table 6 shows the problem assessment data for the three EAP models. Counselors use a two-step process. First, after they complete the assessment, they use a checklist to indicate all of the client's problems. Then they designate one of the assessed problems as the most significant client problem. This choice is a matter of judgment, of course, but staff are comfortable in making this decision. The data in Table 6 describe the most significant client problems.

Evaluation

Table 6
Most Significant Assessed Problem

	External Broadbrush Programs (N = 2,288)	Manufacturing Company (N = 2,597)	Transportation Company (N = 1,673)
Educational/Occupational	2%	7%	3%
Emotional/Mental Health	17%	26%	11%
Financial	5%	2%	3%
Legal	7%	2%	2%
Client Alcohol Use	8%*	9%	42%
Client Drug Use		1%	8%
Family Alcohol Use	9%*	14%	10%
Family Drug Use		1%	3%
Marital	23%	31%*	10%
Family Relationships	13%		4%
Health	1%	2%	1%
Other	15%	5%	3%

*Combined categories

Some interesting differences emerge among the programs. As expected, the transportation company EAP assesses more alcohol or other drug use problems. Combined, client and family alcohol or other drug use problems comprise 63 percent of the caseload. Although counselors assess the full range of problems, the next most frequent category is emotional problems (11%).

The EAP Solution

As indicated earlier, this high rate of alcohol or other drug problem assessment may also be due to characteristics of the employee population. In fact, earlier research has indicated that the transportation company may have a level of alcohol-related job impairment by workers that is nearly twice the national estimate of ten percent.

The other EAPs assess a lower percentage of chemical dependency problems (17% for the external, 25% for the internal). For them the most frequent problems are marital/family, followed by emotional and alcohol or other drug problems. Again, counselors assess the full range of problems.

One should be careful in interpreting these findings. It might be concluded that the transportation company EAP reaches about five times as many alcoholics as the internal broadbrush program (42% vs. 9% assessed client alcohol problems). However, remember that this EAP is seeing 3.2 percent of the work force, compared to eight percent and 5.3 percent for the other programs. Therefore, the actual numbers of assessed alcoholics would be much closer for the same number of eligible employees. As Table 7 shows, the ratio is about two to one rather than five to one, given the same theoretical number of 1,000 eligible employees. Of course, even this comparison is flawed because it assumes two identical employee populations. Still, it does show that *we should keep utilization rates in mind in reviewing comparative data.*

Referral Recommendations

Where the EAP clients are referred is probably the most important process evaluation question. Collectively, the answers determine: 1) the quality and effectiveness of care which clients receive and 2) the health care costs incurred by the company.

Not all clients are referred by the EAPs. Some clients may not need a referral; others may not accept one. Referral data are shown in Table 8. The high use of inpatient/hospital treatment services, outpatient programs, and self-help groups by the transportation company is not surprising. To help contain the company's

Evaluation

Table 7
Theoretical Comparison of Alcoholism Assessment

(In A Work Force Of 1,000 Employees)

Company	Annual Utilization Rate	# Of Clients Annually	% Of Clients Assessed As Alcoholic	# Of Employees Assessed As Alcoholic
Transportation	3.2%	32	42%	13
Manufacturing	8.0%	80	9%	7
Hazelden Contracts	5.3%	53	8%	4

health care costs, EAP staff are utilizing more outpatient services where appropriate and negotiating preferred-provider arrangements with inpatient programs.

The manufacturing company program is unique in that its staff provides short-term clinical counseling (after assessment) to nearly two-thirds of the referred clients. Its rate of inpatient/hospital referrals is much lower at seven percent. This EAP sends only two percent of its referred clients to inpatient/hospital services. This may be because about half of its eligible employees are covered by Health Maintenance Organizations (HMOs) which restrict access to inpatient programs and because the emphasis is on cost containment and early intervention. The external program has the highest utilization of outpatient programs (10%) and private therapists (35%).

Client follow-up data, presented later, are needed to compare the effectiveness of the services used by the three EAPs. However, it is clear that all three programs are doing something in the area of cost containment by using nonresidential providers, negotiating preferred-provider arrangements or by providing the counseling themselves.

The EAP Solution

Table 8
Referrals to Community Resources*

	External Broadbrush Programs (N = 2,288)	Manufacturing Company (N = 2,597)	Transportation Company (N = 1,673)
Inpatient/Hospital	2%	7%	35%
Outpatient Program	10%	5%	7%
Individual, Family or Group Therapy	35%	29%	26%
Self-Help Group	8%	17%	15%
Legal Counseling	11%	4%	2%
Financial Counseling	6%	1%	2%
EAP Clinical Counseling	—	62%	—
Further EAP Assessment	32%**	4%	4%
Other	11%	13%	8%

*Counselors can give more than one referral per client for the broadbrush programs; the percentages do not equal 100%.

**These are referrals of Help Line clients to further (in-person) assessment.

A Closer Look

While it is informative to compare the three EAP models, several questions remain unanswered. How do special populations, such as women or family members, participate in the EAP? Are there differences among employee clients with different occupations? How do different types of employees arrive at the EAP? And do different types of employees have different types of assessed problems?

Evaluation

To examine these questions, further analyses were conducted on Hazelden Employee Assistance data. These data were collected on all 2,712 home office, in-person EAP clients seen between 1983 and 1985. Employee client data were examined first, followed by a comparison of employee and dependent clients.

Employee Referral Sources

Complete employee referral source data are shown in Table 13. Only the major referral patterns are presented here.

- Women are slightly more likely than men to be self-referred (80% vs. 74%). Conversely, women are less likely to be supervisor-referred (8% vs. 13%).
- Blue-collar employees (skilled crafts and labor) are more likely to receive supervisory referrals. White-collar workers (managerial, professional, technical, sales, and clerical) are more likely to be self-referred.
- Employee age and seniority do not appear to affect referral patterns.

Employee-Assessed Problems

As in Table 6, only the data on the most significant client problem — rather than all assessed problems — are analyzed here. The major findings (see Table 14 at the end of this chapter) include

- Assessed problems for male and female employees are much the same except for two categories: emotional and alcohol or other drug problems. Fewer women than men (4% vs. 19%) are assessed with an alcohol or other drug problem. However, more women than men (13% vs. 5%) have an alcohol or other drug problem in the family. Given the lower rates of alcoholism for women, this finding is no surprise. More women (25% vs. 20%) are assessed with emotional problems.
- As employee clients increase in age (and seniority) there is a slow but steady decline in emotional, financial, legal, and marital problems. Family relationship problems increase. The prevalence of both client and family alcohol or other drug problems is relatively unchanged.

- As expected, more married clients than divorced or single clients have marital/personal relationship problems (36% vs. 19% vs. 16%). Married clients are also less likely to have emotional problems.
- Compared to white-collar clients, twice as many blue-collar employees (average 22%) are assessed with alcohol or other drug problems.
- Client alcohol or other drug problems are more prevalent among those clients who are supervisor-referred (29%), than among those who are family (15%) or self-referred (8%). This relationship is reversed for family and marital problems.

Employee and Dependent Comparisons

The previous discussion focused only on employee clients. However, since family members are a significant percentage of the EAP caseload, it is useful to make comparisons between them and the employee clients. It should be pointed out that data are also collected on the eligible employee whose dependent contacted the EAP. Therefore, we can also compare the employees whose families used the EAP with employees who used the program themselves. Their comparative data are at the end of this chapter (see Table 15). The major findings include

- Demographically, dependent clients are very similar to employee clients. The sex ratios are nearly identical. As expected, dependent clients (which include some children) are younger than employee clients.
- Compared to employee clients, dependent clients are more likely to come from families of employees with more seniority. However, employee occupational data are similar for the two groups.
- As expected, referral patterns for the two groups are different. Dependent clients are more likely than employee clients to be family-referred (62% vs. 3%), and less likely to be self-referred (30% vs. 77%). Of course, there are no supervisory referrals for family members.
- In terms of problem assessment, family members have fewer emotional problems (15% vs. 23%) and

more marital/family problems (51% vs. 37%). Otherwise the pattern of assessed problems is similar for both groups.

Overall, there are no surprising differences between employee and dependent EAP clients. Aside from the expected differences in referral patterns and assessed problems, the data on the two groups are similar.

Outcome Evaluation

As stated earlier, outcome evaluation examines the effects or outcomes of a program. The primary question is: Is the client being helped? In addition to EAP client outcomes, the potential economic benefits to the company resulting from the EAP will also be discussed.

Client Outcomes

For the majority of employee assistance clients, assessment/referral counseling is only the first step to getting help. After assessment, most clients are referred to a local provider for help with their problems. We know, for example, that for the three EAPs examined earlier, an average of 91 percent of all EAP clients are referred. But do those clients actually contact the referral? Do their problems improve? And are they satisfied with the services they receive, both from EAP counselors and the provider?

Table 9 shows Hazelden EAP outcome results for the first three quarters of 1985. The data were collected with a questionnaire mailed to clients one month after assessment and referral excluding clients who did not give signed permission, and the response rate is 53 percent. Overall, the data shows that the majority of clients: contact the referral (74%); report their problems are improved (65%); are satisfied with the referral (78%); and are satisfied with the EAP overall (89%).

Other client outcomes can also be measured. The transportation company EAP described earlier also conducts routine EAP client follow-up at three months after assessment and referral excluding clients who did not give signed permission, and the response rate of the telephone interview is 63 percent. Clients who are assessed as alcoholic and referred to treatment are asked

The EAP Solution

Table 9
One-Month Hazelden EAP Client Follow-Up
(N = 395)

Satisfaction With EAP Services	Percentage Of Clients
Counselor was accessible	94%
Counselor was knowledgeable	96%
Problems were kept confidential	95%
Counselor made good recommendations	80%
Overall, EAP services were satisfactory	89%
Experience With Referral	
Received EAP referral	72%
Contacted referral	74%
Satisfied with referral	78%
Problems have improved	65%

about their current alcohol use and Alcoholics Anonymous participation. As Table 10 shows, the majority of clients report abstinence from alcohol (78%) and weekly A.A. attendance (62%). Obviously, these are important outcomes for this program.

Company Outcomes

Cost Containment: Due to skyrocketing corporate health care costs, many companies are also interested in the direct economic benefits resulting from their EAPs. Because EAPs systematically refer employees and dependents to covered services, CEOs are naturally concerned about the impact of the EAP on their benefit programs. The referral data shown earlier (Table 8) indicate that all three EAP models can be successful in containing health care costs. Table 11 shows additional referral data on the Hazelden EAP from an annual report on one of its contracts. About one-third of the

Evaluation

Table 10
Three-Month Follow-Up on Clients Assessed as Alcoholic
(N = 901)

Client Alcohol Use	Percentage Of Clients
Abstinent since EAP contact	78%
Used less than before EAP contact	14%
Used about as much as before EAP contact	7%
Used more than before EAP contact	1%
Client Attendance at Alcoholics Anonymous	
Once a week	62%
Two to three times a month	10%
Once a month	4%
Less than once a month	3%
Do not attend	21%

clients receive no-cost referrals; two-thirds are referred to nonresidential services; only two percent are sent to inpatient programs. While the total cost of these referred services is unknown, it is safe to say that costs would have been higher had employees *not* contacted the EAP and selected providers on their own.

Cost Savings: Beyond short-term cost containment, EAP operations can result in long-term cost savings, principally in the areas of reduced corporate health care utilization and lowered absenteeism. (Savings can also result from improved employee job performance, but this is difficult to measure.) EAP client follow-up data on a Hazelden EAP suggests that cost savings are occurring, as shown in Table 12. Absenteeism and employee use of benefits are lower at follow-up. Finally, significantly fewer employees reported that their jobs are in jeopardy, and more employees reported improved job performance within the last month.

The EAP Solution

Table 11
Referral Recommendations by Hazelden EAP Counselors
(N = 485)

	Percentage Of Referrals
No-Cost Referrals	
EAP counseling only	23%
Self-help groups	9%
Total	32%
Nonresidential Referrals	
Outpatient program	2%
Individual therapy	25%
Family therapy	13%
Group therapy	1%
Legal counseling	9%
Financial counseling	5%
Other	11%
Total	66%
Inpatient Referrals (Chemical Dependency)	
Hospital-based treatment	1%
Freestanding programs	1%
Total	2%

Of course, these findings do not constitute a complete cost-benefit analysis, rather only a "snapshot" of employee behavior before and after EAP contact. Still, it is clear the EAP averts some corporate costs incurred by troubled employees whose problems are causing higher rates of health care utilization, absenteeism, and lowered productivity.

Conclusions

Because the employee populations differ, comparisons among the three EAP models should be viewed with caution. However, some inferences can be made from the process and outcome evaluation data presented here.

1. *Utilization:* Rates are higher for broadbrush models, probably because of their broader focus on all types of personal problems. Utilization is highest for the

Evaluation

Table 12
Comparison of Employee Job Performance Indicators Before and After Contacting the EAP
(N = 109)

Number of:	Use Before	Use After	Amount of Change
Times arrived late for work	196	61	− 135 times
Times left work early	120	43	− 77 times
Times of other absenteeism	56	0	− 56 times
Times used Health Insurance Plan	96	90	− 6 times
Sick days	158	126	− 32 days
Medical leave days*	41	75	+ 34 days
Accidents on the job	2	2	0 days
Times Worker's Compensation used	8	0	− 8 times
Short-term disability	0	0	0 days

*Note: The increase for this item reflects the employee's use of treatment or health care during the four months after the initial contact with the EAP. One would expect the use of this benefit to decrease in the long term.

internal broadbush model, possibly because of its focus *and* location, which may encourage more supervisory referrals.

2. *Penetration:* All three programs show good penetration into their companies and serve a diverse group of employees and their family members.
3. *Early Intervention:* More clients self-refer to the external program. Furthermore, comparisons of presented vs. assessed problems show over half of the clients assessed as chemically dependent initially contact the EAP for a different problem. Together,

these findings suggest the external broadbrush model functions more as an early intervention and prevention program.
4. *Alcohol or Other Drug Assessment:* The transportation company EAP assesses more alcohol and other drug abuse cases than the other EAPs, even with its lower utilization rate. The other EAPs assess more emotional and family/marital problems.
5. *Cost Containment:* All three programs are successful in containing health costs, either by using more outpatient services, by providing short-term counseling, or negotiating treatment costs.
6. *Cost Savings:* Follow-up data on two of the EAPs show both clients and companies are benefiting from the EAP. Clients report they are satisfied with the services they receive and their problems improve. Self-reported data on health claims, work attendance, and performance suggest the EAPs involved are saving their companies money.

As the employee assistance field matures, evaluation and program monitoring will become important to demonstrate effectiveness and quality of care. The basic concepts and methods of program evaluation can be applied to a variety of EAP models. The data from these studies will be different depending on the focus of the EAP. But by examining what we do and what we accomplish, program evaluation can help us maintain and improve our services.

Evaluation

Table 13
Additional Statistical Data
Employee Referral Sources
(N = 2,712)

	Self	Supervisor	Family	Other
Gender				
Male	74%	13%	4%	9%
Female	80%	8%	1%	11%
Age (In Years)				
25 or less	74%	12%	2%	12%
26 to 40	80%	9%	2%	9%
41 to 55	73%	11%	4%	12%
56 or more	73%	11%	1%	15%
Occupation				
Admin/mgmt	82%	7%	3%	8%
Professional	80%	12%	2%	6%
Technical	80%	8%	3%	9%
Sales	74%	8%	3%	15%
Skilled craft	66%	17%	5%	12%
Clerical	75%	10%	2%	13%
Labor	64%	21%	4%	11%
Seniority (In Years)				
One or less	78%	9%	2%	11%
2 to 5	77%	11%	2%	10%
6 to 10	77%	10%	2%	11%
11 to 15	79%	8%	3%	10%
16 to 20	68%	11%	6%	15%
21 or more	82%	6%	4%	8%

The EAP Solution

Table 14
Most Significant Assessed Employee Problem
(N = 2,712)

	Emotional	Finan/ Legal	Client Chem Depend	Family Chem Depend	Marital	Family	Other
Gender							
Male	20%	6%	19%	5%	28%	9%	13%
Female	25%	6%	4%	13%	26%	10%	16%
Age (In Years)							
25 or less	26%	8%	13%	8%	28%	5%	12%
26 to 40	24%	5%	9%	10%	30%	9%	14%
41 to 55	22%	6%	13%	12%	19%	14%	14%
56 or more	19%	4%	13%	8%	15%	20%	21%
Marital Status							
Married	16%	5%	9%	12%	36%	11%	12%
Single	35%	7%	13%	7%	16%	5%	17%
Divorced/sep	28%	8%	10%	9%	19%	14%	12%
Other	46%	3%	11%	6%	9%	14%	11%
Occupation							
Admin/mgmt	15%	4%	10%	8%	29%	13%	21%
Professional	27%	4%	9%	10%	30%	6%	14%
Technical	28%	7%	7%	9%	26%	8%	15%
Sales	26%	2%	12%	7%	30%	10%	13%
Skilled craft	26%	8%	20%	7%	24%	8%	7%
Clerical	24%	8%	6%	14%	26%	10%	12%
Labor	19%	6%	25%	12%	19%	7%	12%
Seniority (In Years)							
One or less	29%	8%	9%	8%	26%	8%	12%
2 to 5	23%	7%	9%	8%	28%	8%	17%
6 to 10	18%	6%	10%	14%	28%	11%	13%
11 to 15	17%	8%	15%	11%	28%	9%	12%
16 to 20	22%	5%	11%	14%	15%	18%	15%
21 or more	22%	2%	7%	14%	14%	21%	19%
Referral Source							
Self	23%	6%	8%	10%	29%	11%	13%
Family member	17%	3%	15%	10%	40%	12%	3%
Supervisor	25%	5%	29%	8%	9%	2%	22%
Other	25%	10%	7%	11%	23%	6%	18%

Evaluation

Table 15
Comparison of Employee and Dependent EAP Clients

	Employees	Dependents
Gender	(N = 2,712)	(N = 1,203)
Male	38%	41%
Female	62%	59%
Age (In Years)		
25 or less	18%	36%
26 to 40	59%	46%
41 to 55	19%	15%
56 or more	4%	3%
Occupation (Of Eligible Employee)		
Administrative/managerial	19%	27%
Professional	9%	9%
Technical	23%	20%
Sales	5%	5%
Skilled craft	9%	11%
Clerical	30%	22%
Unskilled labor	5%	6%
Seniority (Of Eligible Employee)		
One or less	21%	10%
2 to 5	40%	33%
6 to 10	21%	26%
11 to 15	10%	13%
16 to 20	4%	9%
More than 20 years	4%	9%
Referral Source		
Self	77%	30%
Family member	3%	62%
Supervisor	10%	0%
Other	10%	8%
Assessed Problem (Most Significant)		
Emotional	23%	15%
Financial/legal	6%	2%
Client alcohol/drug use	10%	12%
Family alcohol/drug use	10%	12%
Marital	27%	31%
Family	10%	20%
Other	14%	8%

References

Attkisson, C. C., W. A. Hargreaves, M. S. Horowitz, and J. E. Sorensen, *Evaluation of Human Service Programs*, New York, NY, Academic Press, 1978.

Jones, D., *Performance Benchmarks for the Comprehensive Employee Assistance Program*, Center City, MN, Hazelden Educational Materials, 1983, order number 1094.

Patton, M. Q., *Utilization-Focused Evaluation*, Beverly Hills, CA, Sage Publications, 1978.

Schramm, C. J., W. Mandell, and J. Archer, *Workers Who Drink*, Lexington, MA, 1978.

Spicer, J. W., P. Barnett, and D. Kliner, *The Outcomes of Employer Referrals to Treatment*, Center City, MN, Hazelden Educational Materials, 1979.

Spicer, J. W., *Outcome Evaluation: How To Do It*, Center City, MN, Hazelden Educational Materials, 1980.

Spicer, J. W., P. Owen, and D. Levine, *Evaluating Employee Assistance Programs: A Sourcebook for the Administrator and Counselor*, Center City, MN, Hazelden Educational Materials, 1983, order number 1931.

Spicer, J. W., and P. Owen, *Finding the Bottom Line: The Cost Impact of Employee Assistance and Chemical Dependency Treatment Programs*, Center City, MN, Hazelden Educational Materials, 1985.

6
CASE STUDIES

Jerry Spicer, Francis J. Coyne, Thomas Desmond, Robert Ackley, Richard Pine, Morton Aronoff, Henry Huestis, and David Levine.

Francis J. Coyne is Vice President of Human Resources for the Burlington Northern Railroad. Thomas Desmond is the Director of the Johnson & Johnson EAP. Robert Ackley is Director of the Caron Foundation EAP Program, and Richard Pine is Development Director for the Caron Foundation. Morton Aronoff and Henry Huestis are codirectors of the National Broadcasting Company's EAP in New York. David Levine is a Director for Human Affairs International.

HAZELDEN'S EMPLOYEE ASSISTANCE SERVICES
Jerry Spicer, M.H.A.

A Brief History

Like many of Hazelden's programs, employee assistance services were developed in response to community demand and to meet a need in the continuum of

The EAP Solution

care. In the mid-1970s Hazelden was providing consultation to other programs, communities, and businesses, and found an increasing interest in dealing with alcoholism in the workplace. At the same time, there was growing public acceptance of the need for and the effectiveness of chemical dependency treatment and the "Minnesota Model." The federal government was also developing and disseminating information on the concept of employee assistance. These forces culminated in 1976 with Minnesota state legislation providing financial support for employers developing employee assistance programs. This led to Hazelden's initial involvement in the EAP field as a consultant to businesses developing EAPs. For a period of several years Hazelden did not provide direct services to clients, but was involved in establishing several hundred internal and external EAPs and developing some of the EAP literature and training materials in use today.

By the late seventies, the demand for consultation services was decreasing, and interest in having Hazelden deliver EAP services was increasing, with the result that we began delivering a comprehensive range of services to local employers. The next critical point was the development of 1) a system of contracted providers (affiliates), 2) a centralized management information system (SCORE), and 3) a 24-hour toll free telephone (HELP Line) to meet the needs of an employer with employees located throughout the Midwest. This system continues to be expanded as new contracts require the addition of affiliates.

Presently, 75 companies contract for EAP services. Almost 100,000 employees and their families are eligible to use the EAP through our counselors in Minneapolis and St. Paul, the HELP Line, or one of the 100 affiliates we work with in 35 states. Training, communication materials, statistical reporting, and contract management services are part of the typical employee assistance contract. Short-term counseling and benefits consultation/case review are provided to those companies interested in these services.

Case Studies

Hazelden's Employee Assistance Program Philosophy

During the fifteen years Hazelden has been in the EAP field, several decisions about program philosophy have been made: some in anticipation of an issue; some in response to a question. Given the diversity of current approaches in the field, our philosophies are not seen as universal "absolutes," but rather as guidelines that enable us to deliver the quality of service a company wants and is consistent with the overall Hazelden mission.

1. *The Comprehensive Model:* An early decision for Hazelden was whether to focus on occupational alcoholism or on a broader range of personal problems. To some extent the marketplace helped us choose the broader focus, but there were quality of care issues as well. First, we believe alcoholics will present problems other than alcohol or other drug abuse. Having counselors able to assess underlying chemical dependency in a presented problem of family stress enables the identification of alcoholism that might otherwise go undetected for several years. Also, chemical dependency does not exist in isolation from emotional, family, or other problems. Chemical dependency is a primary problem which must be addressed, but Hazelden's goal is improvement in overall quality of life. A multidisciplinary approach to service is required to meet the many needs of our clients. In our experience, the EAP counselor will be seen as a helping resource and cannot turn away employees with problems other than alcohol.

2. *Service Comprehensiveness:* An employee assistance program can be narrowly or broadly focused. Hazelden's stress on Employee Assistance *Services* is intentional for two reasons. First, the needs of the company's management, employees, and families are diverse, and a range of interrelated services will be expected by clients and customers. Second, a danger in not providing training, mailings, etc., is to become only an assessment or telephone hot line service that is probably already available in the

The EAP Solution

community and is not broad enough to meet the needs of the company.

3. *Early Intervention:* The employee assistance program seeks to complement and not duplicate other Hazelden services for the chemically dependent person. Therefore, our EAP focus is on early intervention, job performance, education, and health promotion. As the data in earlier chapters have shown, EAP clients are often self-referred, and we go directly to the employees through our training and communications to encourage use of the EAP. Alcoholism in the work force is a problem requiring more than an EAP. Hazelden's treatment, training, and literature are also part of Hazelden's services for industry.

4. *Potential Conflict of Interest:* The debate about whether a provider of treatment or health care should also provide EAPs will no doubt continue. (Interestingly, this is not a problem the company typically identifies, but rather an issue debated among EAP practitioners). For Hazelden, the central issue is having a check and balance system that addresses a *potential*, but not necessarily an actual problem. These checks include 1) written and monitored quality assurance and case review standards for assessment and referral, 2) open disclosure of referrals (made without identifying clients), 3) a broadly trained staff capable of identifying a range of problems (and not just viewing them as emotional, or psychiatric, or chemical dependency), 4) ongoing reporting and evaluation studies that are made public, 5) clear guidelines for the employer and client on their rights and obligations, and 6) a policy of giving clients more than one referral option, particularly if another Hazelden service is referred to.

5. *The Question of Funding:* As a not-for-profit corporation, Hazelden's activities have a primary objective of helping people and communities. As part of Hazelden, the Employee Assistance Services (EAS) division shares this philosophy and is a not-for-profit enterprise. Conversely, we have taken the position

that employee assistance should be self-supporting and not a "loss leader" where its costs are offset by, for example, patient fees.

In summary, Hazelden's values are not unique or considered as the only way to deliver employee assistance services. Hazelden's commitment to the EAP and chemical dependency fields extends beyond providing direct client services. We have trained several hundred EAP professionals through Hazelden workshops and conferences. The publishing division continues to distribute a variety of written and audiovisual materials on employee assistance. Many strengths have the potential to become problems — for example, being too comprehensive can lead to a dilution of focus and confusion about mission. The major philosophical strength for Hazelden's employee assistance services may be its willingness to review, discuss, and disclose information on the gray areas of service.

Future Challenges

Employee assistance programs will be impacted by changes in employer and employee attitudes and in health care delivery. Maintaining service quality and a consistent program philosophy will be the challenge for Hazelden's Employee Assistance Services. Cost containment, relating to alternative delivery systems (HMOs, PPOs, etc.), drug testing in the workplace, and increasing support for health promotion and wellness are some of the major trends we expect to encounter. At the service level, maintaining consistency throughout a large system of affiliates and keeping the external self-referral emphasis integrated into the workplace are the biggest challenges. The future will be an increasingly competitive and changing EAP environment. For Hazelden, and for all of us, the goal is to provide services consistent with our organizational mission that also meet the needs of our customers and clients.

The EAP Solution

Figure 11
Examples of Hazelden's Employee Assistance Services

Counseling
- assessment
- referral
- follow-up
- short-term counseling

Case Management
- explanation of benefits to employees
- joint conferences with supervisors

Training and Education
- executive briefings
- supervisory trainings
- employee orientations
- special training (e.g., health promotion)

Consultation With Company
- job performance documentation/employee productivity analysis
- benefits design
- special research studies

Employee Communications
- mailings of EAP pamphlets to employees
- posters, wallet cards, etc.
- articles in company newsletters

Health Promotion
- health risk appraisals and employee surveys
- training
- assessment and referral

Service Management
- employee selection, training, and supervision
- affiliate selection and monitoring
- policy and procedure development
- planning and marketing

Evaluation and Research
- quality assurance reviews
- management information system reports
- client satisfaction and follow-up studies
- cost-impact research
- employee surveys

Case Studies

Evolution of the Burlington Northern Employee Assistance Program
Francis J. Coyne

Early History

It is almost impossible to talk about the history of our country without talking at length about the impact of the railroad industry. The remarkable role of the immigrants in developing the natural resources of this country was made possible primarily because of the railroad industry. The tremendous coal resources located in the eastern part of the country, together with the iron ore deposits of northern Minnesota, made mass transportation a necessity if this young country was to become an international industrial force. Names such as Harriman, Hill, and Vanderbilt, to mention only a few, were to make this dream a reality.

It is sometimes forgotten that, while the American railroad industry in its heyday was the largest industry in the world, it was also the most dangerous. Thousands of lives were lost while building major rights-of-way, tunnels, bridges, and structures to ford rivers, lakes, and streams, and to cross mountain ranges. Protective measures such as the Occupational Safety and Health Act (OSHA) and hard hats had not even been conceived in those days. Many of our early industrial accidents happened on railroads.

The danger of this industry increased as the railroad began operating. Here was a production line that operated twenty-four hours a day, seven days a week, in every kind of weather. Derailments, head-on collisions, tail-end collisions, locomotive explosions, and other types of accidents were daily occurrences on most railroads. Loss of life, limb, and health was looked upon as just another cost of doing business. However, as we moved into the twentieth century, public opinion resulted in federal legislation that went to great lengths to protect railroad workers from human and material failures. In fact, laws became so restrictive that it became more economical for the early robber barons to run a safe railroad than to run the most efficient railroad with

The EAP Solution

no consideration for loss of life or limb. At the same time, most railroad workers became organized in various labor union movements, and the unions made safety one of their prime considerations. Because of changes in federal and state laws, demands of workers' organizations, and the commitment of management, the railroads started to become a safer place to work.

However, one major human problem continued that was not dealt with successfully. That was, and continues to be, the problem of on-the-job use and abuse of mood-altering chemicals, including alcohol. The slightest impairment of mental or physical abilities was and still is unacceptable. Railroad managers of those early days were unanimous in their opinion that the single greatest problem they encountered in managing employees was the abuse of, and addiction to, alcohol. It was a subject that did not go unnoticed in the labor union organizations. In fact, many of these organizations preached total abstinence from alcohol. As a result of the use of alcohol by on-duty railroad workers, material and human loss continued and rose to crisis levels.

Management's efforts to control this major problem varied depending upon the individual manager's view of alcohol use. Some managers were punitive and fired everyone they found violating what is referred to as "Rule G." Rule G prohibits the use or possession of alcohol or other mood-altering drugs when an employee is subject to, or is on duty. The net result of this punitive approach was that most employees and some supervisors concealed their co-workers and subordinates' drug use. In their minds, "having a few beers" didn't justify such severe punishment. Those workers who had been fired protested to their unions and were generally successful in returning to work after a reasonable period of punishment. In addition, supervisors and managers also used church counseling, threats, intimidation, and every other kind of cooperative or punitive device. History tells us this was not a successful short- or long-term solution to this age-old problem. Proponents of the "great experiment" of Prohibition were also convinced this was the answer. But again, history taught us otherwise.

Case Studies

The Social Counseling Program

An exciting change occurred in 1935. The Twelve Step program of Alcoholics Anonymous was created. This was the beginning of one of the most miraculous programs known to mankind. In fact, the popular author, Kurt Vonnegut, claims that when history reviews the achievements and contributions of the United States to the well-being of the world, certainly the Twelve Step program of Alcoholics Anonymous will be near the top of any list. And while this chapter is not about Alcoholics Anonymous, the employee assistance movement of today probably would not exist without it.

The period from 1935 to the years following World War II was a period of enlightenment during which alcoholism started to be recognized as a disease that could be identified and successfully treated. For the first time, the stigma of alcoholism began to disappear as the Alcoholics Anonymous movement spread throughout the country. Story after story appeared about the success of treating the "shame" every family tried to hide. The next logical step was for business and industry to recognize that dealing with this age-old problem in such a constructive and successful way could serve their own self-interests.

In 1951 the railroad industry recognized the potential in dealing with its employees as individuals who were suffering from an illness, rather than as employees who were bad and who had failed to follow rules. It was in this year that the Great Northern Railway, under the direction of President John M. Budd, appointed Warren Tangen as the director of an alcohol rehabilitation program — the first in the railroad industry and one of the first in any industry. Tangen hired C. L. Vaughan as his assistant, and together they created a model that was to be refined and used generally throughout industry in this country.

Budd's charge was to create a program using the latest techniques available to treat the use and abuse of alcohol by railroad employees. Approaches that resulted in continued use and cover-up were not acceptable. For want of a better name, the early effort was called the Social Counseling Program. Because of the

The EAP Solution

strong support at top management levels, the program had a good chance for success. A company policy was published that termed alcohol abuse a treatable illness to be handled as a medical rather than moral problem. Procedures were developed that eliminated permanent termination of Rule G violators if they were willing to see the social counselors and follow treatment directives. Successful treatment would result in a return to work with all seniority unimpaired. Training sessions were held at all major locations on the railroad for supervisors, employees, and co-workers. Articles were published in employee magazines and newsletters. Publications were sent to employees' homes so families could become aware of this remarkable new program.

The early referrals were generally late-stage alcoholics who were in trouble on the job and had been referred by their supervisors. Self-referrals started to become more common after employees became convinced of the confidentiality of the program. Many of the early self-referrals, at their first session, initiated conversation with, "I have this *friend* who drinks too much...." At this time, spouse and family referrals also began to increase.

The program was simple in design and concept. Alcoholics Anonymous and, when appropriate, Al-Anon were the primary vehicles used to restore sobriety. Tangen and Vaughan worked with the employees while their wives assisted the spouses and families. There were few treatment centers in those years; most early intervention and counseling was done around the kitchen table. However, two treatment centers used were Hazelden at Center City, MN, and Pioneer House in Minneapolis. Then, as now, involvement with A.A. proved to be the key to successful recovery. In addition, treatment and involvement of the families were critical. Les Vaughan became director of the rehabilitation program upon Tangen's death in 1957, and Kay Vaughan, his wife, became his assistant.

> Obviously an industry or business must operate on the profit motive, or it ceases to exist. However, pre-Twentieth Century methods of "killing the goose to get all the golden eggs" have altered radically. With

the fantastic developments in scientific and technological fields, great strides in medical, health, and welfare programs, and increasingly effective production methods, it has been necessary to take a new look at the one constant factor untouched through all this change. This is the human factor. All the technical equipment in the world is useless without skilled men and women to operate it. Therefore, an industry must include in its main purpose of profit, the deepest concern for its most important asset — its employees.

The above paragraph is taken from a report written by Les Vaughan in 1961. It summarized the company's Rehabilitation Program for Alcoholics and Problem Drinkers since its inception in 1951. Although the intent sounds mild compared to present standards, in 1961 this new policy was controversial. Vaughan went on to report: "As of this date, 1,223 cases have been handled. Ten years' summation indicates approximately 750 satisfactory recoveries (presenting no further problems to the company). Approximately 150 have shown little or no improvement and are still problems though still working. The balance of 323 include those permanently dismissed or deceased." These are not bad results for a program that many predicted would fail.

The program had proven itself to be economically beneficial and accepted by employees, labor organizations, and management. This basic philosophy — primary treatment where necessary, affiliation with Alcoholics Anonymous, and personal contact and encouragement from the railroad counselors — continued over the next two decades. By the fall of 1981, the department had grown to consist of a director and ten counselors. Mergers with other railroads had changed the company name to Burlington Northern and had increased the number of employees in the work force to 57,000. Approximately 4,800 employees had received help from the Social Counseling Program.

The Employee Assistance Program

The year 1981 was critical for the program. Employee feedback indicated a rather large group of employees

The EAP Solution

was not using the program because they feared they would be labeled "alcoholic." Even though counselors' offices were located off-property, there was real concern on the part of employees that they would be known as someone who used the "alcoholic's program." Although today it might be perceived to have been easy to change the alcohol-only program to a full comprehensive employee assistance program, that was not the case. The program director at that time was committed to dealing with alcohol cases only and resigned when plans were made to change the composition of the program. The Employee Assistance Program was ultimately expanded to include other employee problems that could affect job performance. Counselor training was upgraded, and employees were encouraged to use the services of the EAP counselors for a wide range of living problems. Alcohol was just one of those problems; others were finances, legal difficulties, marriage, stress, and other personal problems affecting job performance. The results, of course, were predictable. From 1981 to 1985 the caseload more than doubled (Figure 12). In addition, the alcohol and chemical dependency cases increased by about the same percentage. Employees were more apt to talk to a counselor about safe subjects, such as marriage, finance, etc., but upon investigation, the problems often stemmed from alcohol or other drug abuse. Even though the work force was declining during this period, the penetration rate of the EAP program actually tripled from one and a half percent to over five percent. Many more early-stage chemical abusers were being treated.

The need to contain costs of health care programs was the other crucial factor during this period. Under the alcohol-only program, effective in 1981, 76 percent of all alcoholism and chemical dependency clients were referred to very expensive inpatient treatment. This percentage has now declined to only 25 percent in 1985, with many more clients being referred directly to self-help or outpatient programs which are substantially less costly. Another area of cost containment was to negotiate individually with treatment centers used for preferred provider contracts. Through this procedure,

**Figure 12
E.A.P. Caseload**

☐ CD Cases
■ Total Cases
▨ Treatment Referrals (Inpatient)

Year	CD Cases	Total Cases	Treatment Referrals (Inpatient)
1981	744	974	744
1983	1049	1500	675
1984	1045	1675	575
1985	1319	2038	522

Burlington Northern Railroad

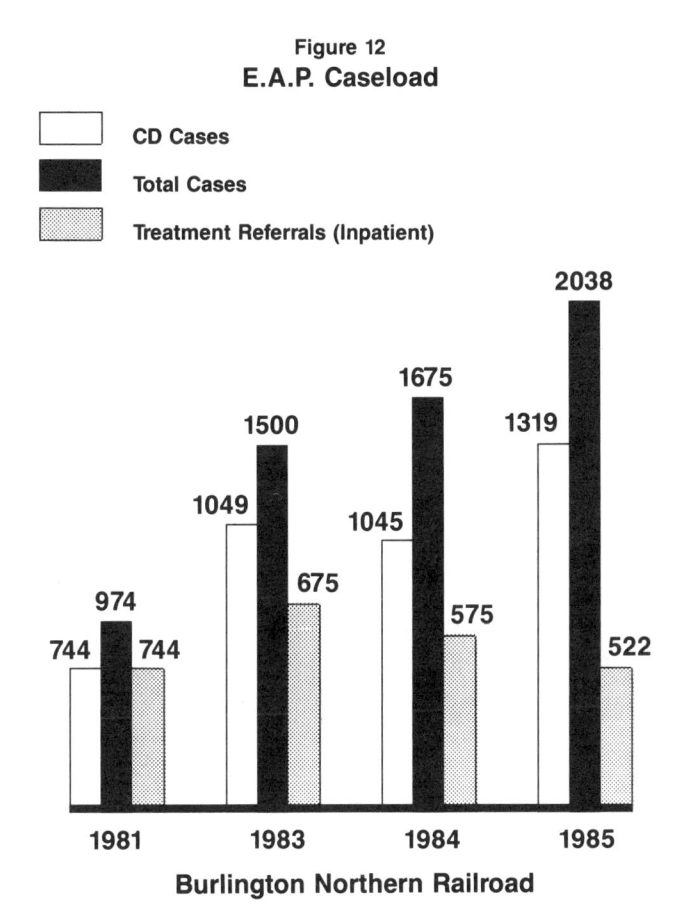

Burlington Northern was able to reduce the cost of inpatient treatment about twenty percent. The total annual savings through cost-containment programs and referral of more clients to outpatient and self-help groups amounted to over a million and a half dollars from 1981 to 1985.

Critical to everything we do in the Employee Assistance Program is the number of clients who are making satisfactory recovery after EAP counseling. Our measure of satisfactory recovery is that the client present no further problems to the company. For the first ten years of the Employee Assistance Program, 61 percent of the clients presented no further problems. This success ratio increased to 77 percent in 1983 and 78 percent in

The EAP Solution

1984 (Figure 13). We monitor these numbers very carefully to insure the recovery rates continue to be maximized. We are convinced the early detection of alcoholism through the "safe" subjects such as stress, marital, financial, or other problems, allows us to see clients at a much earlier stage of their drinking career than in the past. Because of this early detection, the need for inpatient care is dramatically reduced.

Figure 13
C/D Cases

Satisfactory Recovery
(Presenting No Further Problems to the Company)

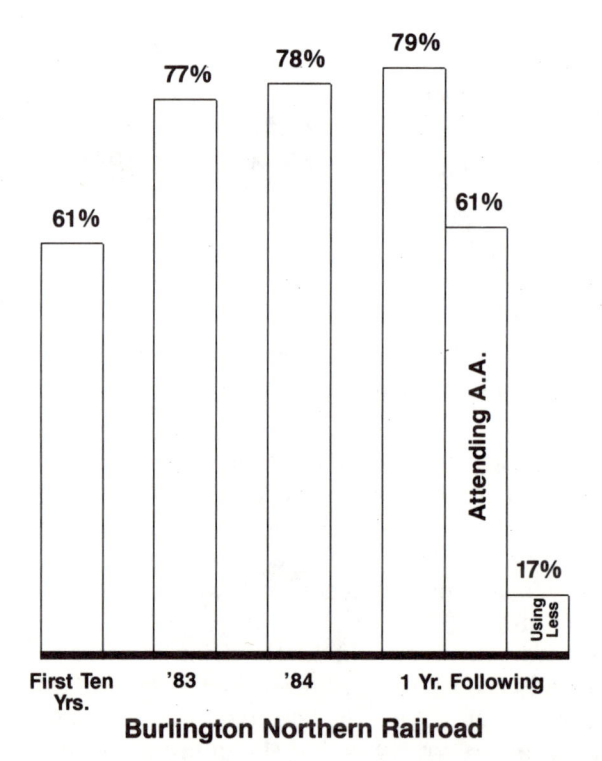

	First Ten Yrs.	'83	'84	1 Yr. Following
	61%	77%	78%	79%
Attending A.A.				61%
Using Less				17%

Burlington Northern Railroad

The confidentiality and the acceptance of our program continue to be reinforced. In the last twelve months, 60 percent of our EAP clients said they came to us for help either on their own or at the request of their

Case Studies

family. The remainder contacted the program because of the concern of their supervisors (before job performance problems), on the advice of friends, or because of discipline for rule infractions involving alcohol or other drugs. Others came because of doctors, clergy, trouble with law enforcement, etc. A recent employee attitude survey indicated a very high degree of confidence in both the success and confidentiality of the Burlington Northern Employee Assistance Program.

From an economic standpoint, the program continues to reward the company in terms of less use of health insurance, on-time arrival, etc., as indicated in Table 16.

Table 16
Job Performance Changes

Indicators (Previous Month)	At Intake	At 3 Month Follow-Up	At 12 Month Follow-Up
Used health insurance	17%	8%	5%
Arrived late for work	17%	5%	3%
Left work early	13%	4%	3%
Took sick days	18%	7%	8%
Used medical leave	4%	7%	4%
Job in jeopardy	25%	7%	4%

Burlington Northern Railroad

Operation Stop

A current thrust of the Employee Assistance Program is toward prevention. Our efforts in this area, entitled OPERATION STOP, began in January 1985. Local committees throughout the company are made up of labor union members. Local union chairmen provide a resource list of employee volunteers from various locations

The EAP Solution

who are interested in creating a drug-free work environment. These volunteers are brought to a two-day training session where alcoholism and other chemical dependencies are discussed in detail. They learn how they might go about creating a safe environment in their work locations. The training consists of leadership skills, communication skills, an overview of the Employee Assistance Program, and training in how to confront co-workers who may be using chemicals in an inappropriate manner. Over 425 volunteers were trained during 1985 and are operational at 60 different locations. Efforts at expanding the program continue.

Early indications are that these peer committees are being accepted and that their presence is creating an environment where co-workers no longer condone the use of drugs at work. Safer work environments, healthier lifestyles, and reduced problems relating to inappropriate use of chemicals on the job are becoming more common. The design of the program allows the committees to promote OPERATION STOP through baseball caps, T-shirts, bumper stickers, bulletin board announcements, softball tournaments, and other employee activities that create an awareness of the importance of this role. Union leaders have strongly supported and been involved in the OPERATION STOP program.

While committees are autonomous, they are encouraged to develop a working relationship with the local management to whom they report on their regular jobs. The prevention group publishes a periodic newsletter called *The Messenger. The Messenger* is designed to promote OPERATION STOP, inform employees of committee activities, and keep them aware of efforts that help create this safe environment.

Rule Changes and Medical Approach

At the same time, management has relaxed the punitive aspects of Rule G violations. No longer are employees pulled out of service and told to report to the EAP counselor. Now the employee remains in service if he or she cooperates with the EAP counselor and is removed only for lack of cooperation. If employees are involved in accidents or rule violations, they are required to submit to a urinanalysis. If it is positive, again no punitive action is taken if the employee cooperates with the EAP counselor. The Medical Department is also requiring urinanalysis in ongoing physical examinations of our employees. Again, positive tests require cooperation with the EAP counselor. In the above instances, if inpatient treatment is prescribed, appropriate leaves of absence are granted. Second Rule G violations result in permanent dismissal.

Conclusion

Can we now say that the problem of drugs in the workplace is solved? Of course not. Have we gone to every extent possible to deal with one of the most complex and pervasive human problems facing modern society? Probably not. Do we have a reasonable approach to a problem that may never be solved entirely? The answer to this question is a definite YES.

The foundations of the program are simple and constructive.

1. Rule G is strictly enforced. Any violation of the rule is deemed very serious and unacceptable behavior.
2. Discipline for first-time Rule G violators is positive and therapeutic. This applies both to those social users who make an error in judgment and to those who have lost all ability to control the use of mood-altering chemicals. Treatment ranges from attending DWI seminars to inpatient counseling.
3. Chemical dependency is treated the same as other disabilities. Early identification and treatment are encouraged.
4. Probable cause and medical testing are used where appropriate with no punitive action taken as long as employees cooperate with the EAP counselor.
5. Voluntary referrals to the EAP program are assured strict confidence.
6. Our overall approach is neither pro-union nor anti-union but pro-employee.

Our program continues to be dynamic. When and if future changes are indicated, they will be made.

An Internal Broadbrush Program Johnson & Johnson's Live for Life® Assistance Program
Thomas C. Desmond, Ed.D.

Evolution

Johnson & Johnson is the most diversified health care corporation in the world. It grosses over $6.5 billion a year and employs approximately 75,000 employees at 165 companies in 56 countries. Its philosophical base is embodied in a document called "Our Credo." A section of this document makes a commitment to the welfare of its employees.

The Johnson & Johnson companies are decentralized and directly responsible for their own operation. Corporate management is committed to maintaining this decentralization because of the many proven advantages to the businesses and people involved.

Because of the success of a pilot employee assistance program launched in 1978 at Ethicon, a Johnson & Johnson subsidiary, and our commitment to the principles in the Credo, Johnson & Johnson decided to implement internal employee assistance programs throughout the Family of Companies wherever they were feasible. Because of the need to respect the autonomy of each company, it was decided that the development of consortia of our own companies would be in keeping with our philosophy of decentralization and would give effective employee assistance services to Johnson & Johnson employees and their family members. The consortium approach was developed in early 1980 and took approximately five years to implement. It was completed in 1985.

More than 90 percent of all domestic employees now have direct access to an employee assistance program with the remaining employees having telephone access. There are employee assistance programs at all major Johnson & Johnson locations throughout the United States, Puerto Rico, and Canada. Programs are also operating in Brazil and England. The smaller Johnson & Johnson companies not in a consortium area are serviced by consultants. All Johnson & Johnson employee

Case Studies

Table 17
Live for Life Assistance Program
Growth Pattern Within Family of Companies

	Number of Employees and Locations Having Access to EAP						
	1979	1980	1981	1982	1983	1984	1985
North America	2,600	10,900	16,950	23,770	26,940	28,500	30,550
International	—	5,500	5,500	6,700	6,700	8,300	8,300
Employees	2,600	16,400	22,450	30,470	33,640	36,800	38,850*
Locations	(1)	(6)	(29)	(54)	(58)	(63)	(70)

*A reduction in the worldwide work force took place between 1983-85.

Johnson & Johnson

assistance-administrated programs and most consultant programs are in-house.

The marketing of the employee assistance program throughout the Johnson & Johnson Family of Companies was accomplished in three phases. The first phase was contact with the managers and directors of personnel. A needs assessment was executed and an educational process was initiated to inform these managers and directors about the employee assistance program. This EAP training was then conducted throughout each Personnel Department. The second phase was a formal presentation to the management board of each company. This phase included both information about the employee assistance program and an alcohol and other drug education component for executives. The third phase was the development of cost estimates and the actual employment of an EAP administrator to implement the program.

The corporate director of the employee assistance programs screened all candidates as to their professional qualifications. Because of the needs of the program, all candidates were required to have at least a master's degree, experience in both the chemical dependency and mental health fields, therapeutic skills, and some familiarity with the business setting. Because of the autonomy of each program, candidates needed to exhibit a high energy level and evidence of being self-starters. After the initial screening, final candidates were interviewed on-site by all appropriate members of management to ascertain how they would fit within the culture of the company(ies) for which they were candidates. Final selection resided with the management of the individual companies.

The Program

The Johnson & Johnson employee assistance program offers employees and family members confidential, professional assistance for problems related to alcohol and other drugs, marital, family, emotional, and/or mental health problems which could be adversely affecting them. The Johnson & Johnson employee assistance programs reflect the evolution of the employee assistance program movement which began with the founding of Alcoholics Anonymous in the mid-thirties, the occupational alcoholism programs of the forties and fifties, and the comprehensive broadbrush programs of today. They incorporate the holistic philosophy of Alcoholics Anonymous that people's problems are physical, mental, and spiritual (in a nonreligious sense, i.e., self-worth, relationships with fellow human beings) in nature. The treatment of the whole person is the philosophical base of the counseling effort. The treatment goal is to help clients assume responsibility for their own behavior and, if it's destructive to themselves or others, to modify it. This process is supported with a variety of therapeutic modalities which clearly recognize that any one therapy is not a panacea for the resolution of the client's problem(s). The employee assistance program is committed to a multimodal approach in both the assessment of problems and the course of treatment.

Furthermore, Johnson & Johnson's employee assistance program is publically committed to identify and remedy the number one social health problem in our country — substance abuse and addiction. The program is specifically designed to actively identify, intervene, and treat substance abuse and addiction as well as the family disease of alcoholism and other drug addiction.

The program also emphasizes the necessity of maintaining complete confidentiality when counseling the employee or family member in order to protect both the client's dignity and job.

Cost Containment and Evaluation

The low ratio of one administrator to approximately 1,500 employees makes it possible to have a substantive in-house counseling program. A study of Johnson & Johnson's employee assistance program in the New Jersey area showed that clients with drug, emotional, or mental health problems who availed themselves of these EAP counseling services were counseled at substantial savings to the company.

Another cost-containment process which has been implemented throughout the Family of Companies is the referral protocol to outside community resources.

This protocol gives guidelines as to referral of clients to inpatient and outpatient treatment. As a result of implementing these guidelines throughout the system, inpatient treatment referrals are between six and seven percent of our total referrals. This represents substantial savings in medical benefit payments as compared to employee and family members who did not use the service.

The employee assistance program has been monitored since its inception. In 1984, this monitoring system became formalized with the contracting of the Hazelden System for Computerized Reporting and Evaluation (SCORE). Both corporatewide and individual company quarterly and annual reports are issued. Baseline benchmarks have been set up throughout the corporation in which all employee assistance administrators are asked to monitor their programs. Some of the more important benchmarks are a supervisory referral rate of from fifteen to twenty percent of referral sources; an alcohol or other drug assessment rate of

The EAP Solution

Figure 14
Live For Life® Assistance Referral Guidelines
Criteria for Referral By Live For Live Assistance

A. Alcohol and Other Drug Abuse
  1. Outpatient referral
  Referral to Certified Alcoholism Counselors, psychiatrists, psychologists, M.S.W., family and marriage counselors, financial, legal, and EAP counselors or agencies furnishing these kinds of services.
     a. when client is physically able to withdraw from alcohol or other drugs safely
     b. when no psychosis, other than drug induced, appears to be present
     c. when there is no history of repeated relapses
     d. when current lifestyle supports recovery process
  2. Inpatient referral
     a. when a nondrug-induced psychosis appears to be present or there is a history of psychosis
     b. threat of suicide or other types of life-threatening situations
     c. when client is physically unable to withdraw from alcohol or other drugs safely
     d. when client has repeated relapses on an outpatient basis
     e. when current lifestyle would interfere with recovery process
     f. consultation with Health Department physician prior to admission where physician is available
     Note: If conditions c, d, and e only exist, residential nonhospital base of treatment could be appropriate.

B. Emotional Problems
  1. Outpatient referral
  Referral to psychiatrists, psychologists, M.S.W., family and marriage counselors, financial, legal, EAP counselors or agencies furnishing these kinds of services.
     a. emotional problems which are behavioral or phobic in nature
     b. marital or family problems or both
     c. adolescents or children
  2. Inpatient referral
     a. acute behavioral change such as hallucinations and bizarre behavior
     b. threat of suicide or other types of life-threatening situations
     c. when a patient is not responding to outpatient treatment
     d. consultation with Health Department physician prior to admission where physician is available

Johnson & Johnson

from 20 to 25 percent of significant problems; a family member caseload share of from fifteen to twenty percent; and inpatient referrals of between five and seven percent of all referrals. Other indicators are assessed, such as the penetration of various population groups such as minorities, wage and salaried employees, and various departments throughout the system. Program promotional efforts are modified to respond to this information. The most important indicator of program activity is the utilization rate benchmark, which is from five to ten percent.

Johnson & Johnson's employee assistance program utilization rate is seven percent for new family units. This rate has been constant since the inception of the program. The computation of this rate is based on the employee population and each family unit first entering into the system. In order for a case to be included in the annual utilization rate, the client must be the first member of the employee's family unit to utilize the employee assistance program. An Initial Client Questionnaire and Assessment/Referral form is completed, and a control number is assigned. Once an employee family unit is entered into the system, it is never counted again in the utilization rate. Supervisory and management consultations are not counted in the utilization rate.

A Quality Assurance Program has been initiated which will review all programs on a biennial basis. The Quality Assurance Team is chaired by the Corporate Director of Assistance Programs, and its members consist of outside consultants expert in the fields of employee assistance and mental health.

Live for Life and the Future

During the employee assistance program's developmental period, substantial programs were being developed in the fields of health and safety. In 1977 the Chairman of the Board of Johnson & Johnson made a commitment to provide all employees and their families with the opportunity to become the healthiest employees of any corporation in the world. The first step to achieving this goal was to create LIVE FOR LIFE. Strategy was developed to create a corporate culture thoroughly supportive of good health practices. Preventative health component action programs were implemented such as exercise, cessation of smoking, stress management, nutrition, and weight control. Within two years, those companies which participated in LIVE FOR LIFE showed a 23 percent quit rate for smokers and an eleven percent increase in cardiovascular fitness.

In 1980, Industrial Hygiene developed an environmental surveillance and control program for the recognition, evaluation, and control of potential workplace chemical and physical health hazards.

The EAP Solution

**Figure 15
Cumulative Utilization Rate
Johnson & Johnson Employee Assistance Programs**

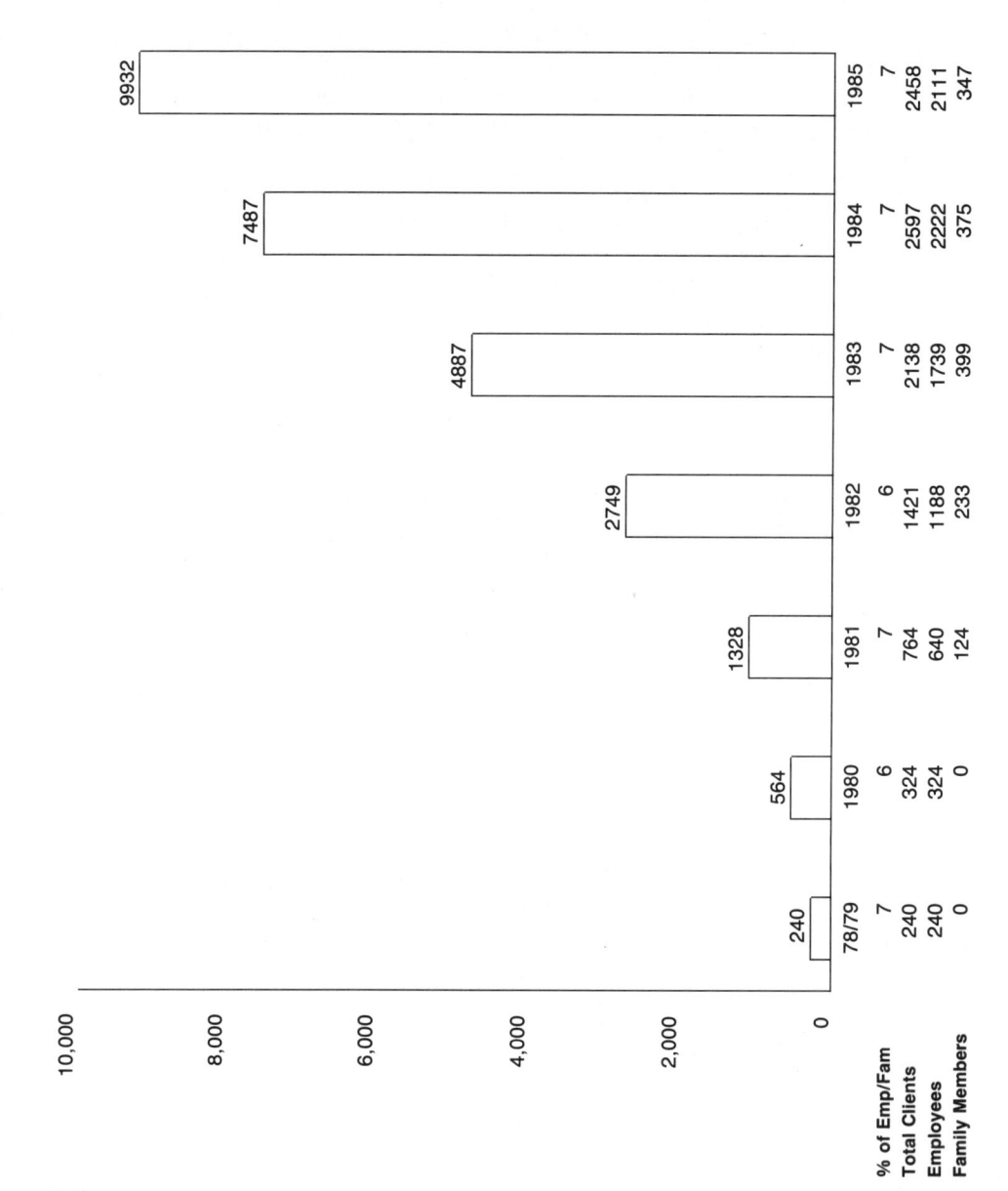

	78/79	1980	1981	1982	1983	1984	1985
% of Emp/Fam	7	6	7	6	7	7	7
Total Clients	240	324	764	1421	2138	2597	2458
Employees	240	324	640	1188	1739	2222	2111
Family Members	0	0	124	233	399	375	347

Cumulative values shown on bars: 240, 564, 1328, 2749, 4887, 7487, 9932

Case Studies

Medical and Occupational Health Nursing developed a computerized Employee Health Profile which was an educational and referral mechanism. Medical surveillance programs for the employees were developed in conjunction with the industrial hygiene environmental surveillance and control programs. A co-consultation process between Medical and Employee Assistance was implemented to assure high quality care for our employees.

Corporate Benefits adapted insurance premiums to encourage lifestyle changes (reduced life insurance rates for nonsmokers, weight loss, use of seat belts, fire extinguishers in the home, lower cholesterol rates, and hypertension control). Hospitalization deductibles were waived for employees who used the employee assistance program to deal with alcohol or other drug problems.

A safety program effort was initiated in 1980 which addressed the reduction of Lost Work Day Cases. During this period, and as a result of these efforts, the Lost Work Day Case rate was reduced by 90 percent. A stringent corporatewide fire/safety policy was implemented and a new Fleet Safety Program adopted to reduce the fleet accident rates. This program embodies a "No Drinking and Driving" policy.

As a result of these programs, it became evident there were synergies to be gained by a more closely integrated process and working relationship among the different employee health disciplines. Employee assistance administrators were invited to be a part of the fleet accident review boards, and nurses were trained to identify drug and mental health problems. Wellness coordinators and benefits administrators were also sensitized to identify and refer employees with personal problems. Joint meetings were held with Corporate Benefits and Employee Assistance Program administrators to review health benefits, and modifications were made where necessary. Other cooperative activities were initiated such as health fairs, management training seminars, employee orientations, and education programs.

In 1986 all these health-related programs were linked together under the aegis of LIVE FOR LIFE and made

The EAP Solution

available to each of the employees and to their family members. This partnership benefits the employee and the family as well as the company and promotes greater utilization of all the services. Employee assistance programs, the employees' benefits program, the Medical Department, Environmental Health and Safety, and LIVE FOR LIFE are now LIVE FOR LIFE Assistance Program, LIVE FOR LIFE Benefits, LIVE FOR LIFE Medical, LIVE FOR LIFE Safety, and LIVE FOR LIFE Wellness. The new LIVE FOR LIFE is the ultimate expression of the Johnson & Johnson Family of Companies' 1977 commitment to provide the best possible health care for their employees. This LIVE FOR LIFE active health partnership contains a comprehensive group of health-related services which offer employees and family members the opportunity to maximize their health and well-being. This new partnership is a coordinated way of communicating and delivering all health-related programs so the employee and family member can benefit from the linkage of all the health-related services.

And the Johnson & Johnson LIVE FOR LIFE Assistance Program is a full partner in this landmark effort in occupational health.

Treatment Providers and EAP Consulting: Mutually Exclusive?

Robert J. Ackley, Ph.D.
Richard M. Pine, M.B.A.

An issue of concern in most professional environments is conflict of interest. Nowhere is this more apparent or more hotly debated than in the provision of human services. One of the purposes of this chapter is to explore the issue of chemical dependency treatment centers and other health care providers offering employee assistance program services to business and industry. Critics claim there is an inherent conflict of interest, that the primary motivation of treatment providers is to channel referrals and income into their treatment services. Proponents believe EAP services represent another element in the full continuum of care. Clearly, there are a great many relevant concerns.

Pros and Cons of Treatment Centers Providing EAP Services

Those who advocate the provision of EAP services by treatment providers make a number of claims to support their position. Because business and industry are increasingly concerned about substance abuse in the workplace, chemical dependency treatment providers, with their specific expertise in the area of addictions, are in a unique position to provide both employee assistance and treatment services. EAP practitioners who also provide counseling or treatment services claim they are meeting the needs of many organizations by "one-stop shopping," where companies are able to arrange for both EAP and treatment services in one package. Under such arrangements, companies are often able to purchase treatment services at a preferred rate. Because EAP services are another element in an overall continuum of client care, proponents of this position claim that a higher percentage of clients will accept treatment referrals. In addition, both follow-up and integration of the employee reentering the workplace tend to be more efficient and consistent. Therefore, it is argued that the client is better served when EAP services, treatment, and follow-up are all provided by the same individual or agency.

Critics of this issue believe there is an inherent conflict of interest when EAP services are provided by treatment professionals. Because they have a strong interest in referring clients to their practices or treatment centers, it is argued a truly objective assessment of client needs cannot take place. Some even say the individual diagnosis may be inadvertently, or even intentionally, pointed in the direction of the illness or problem in which the provider specializes. Critics also believe persons representing a particular treatment resource tend to have specific training in one area but lack the broad base of expertise necessary to provide effective EAP services. For example, it is argued that persons representing chemical dependency treatment centers have expertise in addictions but often are not trained in working effectively with clients suffering from other personal difficulties. Conversely, groups of private therapists often have expertise in mental health and psychological issues but do not have sufficient expertise in chemical dependency to work effectively in the employee assistance field. Critics argue that persons representing treatment centers compete unfairly in the EAP marketplace. They may underbid for an EAP contract with the intention of recouping their losses from fees collected from clients referred to their treatment facilities. Therefore, critics claim independent providers of employee assistance services are unfairly disadvantaged. A related argument by critics is that treatment providers are often able to provide substantial financial backing to their employee assistance efforts from funds generated through their treatment facilities. It is often claimed that independent EAP practitioners have no outside source of funding and this constitutes unfair competition and puts independent EAP practitioners at a specific disadvantage.

Additional points could be made on both sides of this complex issue. However, it appears the overriding concern in these arguments is whether conflict of interest is occurring, and, if so, who may be disadvantaged by such an arrangement.

Case Studies

Conflict of Interest

In most conflict of interest situations, one party tends to benefit while another is disadvantaged in some way. For example, a few chemical dependency treatment centers have been known to pay for referrals by awarding gifts, cash, trips, and other "perks" to regular referral sources. An EAP professional at a large company was recently offered a week at a beachfront condominium for the possibility of future referrals. The winners in this situation are the treatment provider and the referral source, while the loser is the client/employee who may have been inappropriately referred to treatment. Other treatment centers who refuse to buy referrals in this manner are also losers, since they may be denied appropriate referrals.

Conflict of interest issues are frequently raised in other fields. Financial planners, for example, often represent themselves as independent when they are affiliated with an agency or a company that advocates a set of financial products. The client who is looking for strictly objective financial advice may be disadvantaged since the financial planner has specific monetary interest in pushing his or her products to the exclusion of others that may be more appropriate.

There is a direct analogy between this type of conflict of interest and that in the EAP field. When human resource treatment providers (including chemical dependency treatment centers or counselors or both, psychologists, psychiatrists, social workers or other therapists) market and provide EAP services to business and industry, there is significant potential for conflict of interest. When EAP treatment providers have a primary interest in referring clients to their own practices or treatment centers, a truly objective assessment of client needs is difficult. As in the other conflict of interest scenarios previously discussed, the disadvantaged party is the client or employee who may be inappropriately referred to one form of treatment to the exclusion of others that may be a better solution.

Potential Versus Actual Conflict of Interest

It is clear that a strong potential for conflict of interest exists in many situations, both in the EAP field and

The EAP Solution

in any situation where services are provided to consumers. Is it possible for treatment providers to offer EAP services to business and industry and still provide fully objective assessments of clients' needs? Stated differently, the key issue is whether the EAP professional can meet the needs of the employee and employer while still being responsible to the treatment provider he or she represents.

One way to address this question directly is to determine the motivation, objectives, and qualifications of the provider who proposes to offer employee assistance services on a consulting or contractual basis. James T. Wrich presented the issue in this way:

> The consultant's primary objective should be to develop a program which will move people with problems into the appropriate continuum of care. We reject efforts on the part of those care-givers whose consultations lack professionalism and are mainly geared to fill their own treatment beds. Being able to successfully assist chemically dependent or other troubled employees to recover from their problems does not necessarily qualify (one) to help a company and union develop a successful joint program.... Even people with professional qualifications in health care delivery will fail if they have not been adequately prepared in the specific field of occupational program development.... The question to be answered is whether the consultant's primary objective is to develop an employee assistance program which will serve the interests of the employer, the union, and the employees, or if it's just to funnel the clients to himself or to a particular rehabilitation program. While the latter is not necessarily unethical or contrary to the best interests of the employer, *it could be*. It is necessary to reach a clear understanding of what the long-term relationship will be between the employer and the consultant, and *the best interest of the client should be the determining factor*. (emphasis added)*

---

*James T. Wrich, *The Employee Assistance Program Updated For the 1980's*, Hazelden Educational Materials, 1980.

Two points are particularly important here. First, the provision of EAP services by treatment centers or other human resource persons presents a *potential* conflict of interest situation, not necessarily an *actual* conflict of interest. Second, and more important, because the client or employee is the disadvantaged person in a conflict of interest situation, the *best interest* of the client should always be the primary consideration in selecting an EAP provider. We should ask: What are the qualifications of the EAP provider? What are the objectives of the two contracting parties, and are these objectives openly shared with one another? And, finally, how will the best interests of the clients be assured? If these three questions can be satisfactorily answered, it matters little who provides the EAP services or with whom that individual or organization is associated.

"Behind the Scenes" Issues

Clearly, the majority of professionals who have raised conflict of interest issues have done so out of a conscientious and sincere concern regarding the integrity of their profession and a dedicated commitment to the best interests of their clients.

But as with any other industry attracting new competition, there may be a few others concerned with the potential erosion of their own competitive positions in the marketplace. The U.S. automobile market is one example. As the products from Japan began to cut more deeply into their share of the domestic market, calls for import quotas and concerns about trade deficits abounded. Was not the real concern the inability of U.S. manufacturers to achieve and maintain competitive advantage?

In the chemical dependency treatment field, we have seen hospital-based programs being developed as new competition for older, well-established free-standing facilities. We heard claims such as, "They're only interested in filling unused beds," or "Where were they when there wasn't money to be made from a drug and alcohol unit?" At least in part, was there not also a concern about the community recognition and credibility with which these other health care providers were

The EAP Solution

entering the market, and the advantage that provided them?

There may be similarities regarding the issue of the treatment providers and employee assistance services. In many communities, the hospital or rehabilitation center that is developing EAP services has several key marketplace advantages:

1. existing key corporate and community contacts and relationships
2. in-house marketing expertise and promotional capabilities
3. greater access to capital

These factors, if they exist, do not by themselves constitute unfair competition, but rather a positional advantage within the market. It would behoove the independent EAP practitioners to evaluate their strengths and weaknesses relative to their competitors and then develop appropriate marketing and business strategies to effectively compete.

It appears both providers and consumers of employee assistance services can adequately address, if not resolve, conflict of interest questions by continuing to develop and refine guidelines and criteria for selecting and operating a viable, professional employee assistance program.

Guidelines for Selecting an EAP Provider

The following guidelines are relevant both to companies interested in selecting an EAP and also to treatment providers wishing to offer EAP services to business and industry. While these guidelines do not insure conflict of interest will be eliminated, they provide a structure that will greatly reduce the potential for clients to be disadvantaged by a conflict of interest situation.

1. Determine the *primary motive* of EAP providers in offering services. Are they primarily in the business to fill treatment beds, or are they committed to developing quality, broadbrush service that has financial independence from treatment services? Feel free to ask the providers questions about their sources of funding.

Case Studies

2. Determine the overall *quality of EAP services* you will be receiving. The specific experience of EAP providers is probably the most relevant variable in quality of service. Do the providers have training and experience in both addictions and counseling for other types of personal concerns? Are they experienced in EAP design, implementation, administration, and evaluation? Do you like the providers? Are they reasonably warm and appropriate, or aloof and distant? Finally, does the program meet acceptable standards, such as those endorsed by ALMACA?
3. Know your *main objectives* in desiring an EAP service. To what degree will the EAP providers tailor the program to meet your needs? Do your objectives match the motives and objectives of the providers? Do the providers have the expertise to offer the variety of services you require?
4. Decide whether the *best interests of employees* are served by this EAP provider. In spite of ties to a particular treatment program, do you believe the provider can offer a strictly objective assessment of client needs? An important factor to consider is whether the EAP provider is evaluated by their company strictly on EAP performance, or on the number of referrals made to the treatment program. In addition, a typical warning sign of conflict of interest is an exceptionally low fee for EAP services. It is important to determine whether the provider expects to recover losses through fees generated from treatment referrals, or whether fees are reduced for other reasons (e.g., fewer services offered, provider willing to make minimal profit for the benefit of developing a company contract in a particular geographical area). Ultimately, the question to ask is: "In what way might my employees be hurt or disadvantaged by the services this provider offers?"
5. Ask potential EAP providers for *references*. Are they serving other companies in your area? If not, their treatment referral network may be minimal and may need substantial development. Talk to personnel at other companies. Discuss your concerns openly, particularly regarding potential conflict of interest and the willingness of the providers to show flexibility in meeting your needs.

The EAP Solution

Suggestions for Treatment Providers Offering EAP Services

As more treatment providers decide to offer EAP services to business and industry, guidelines are necessary for the structuring of these programs to protect the interests of both employees and employers.

1. The EAP service should operate *independently* of the treatment component. The service should have its own budget and planning process, as well as control over its decision making. In this way, the EAP service is developed to stand on its own as a separate business unit.
2. *Goals and objectives* for the EAP service should be clearly defined by way of a complete business plan, including financial projections, break-even analysis, and the development of a structure to achieve profitability.
3. *Experienced EAP personnel* should be responsible for the EAP service. Knowledge in the various aspects of EAP development, administration, and evaluation are important, as well as counseling skills. Assigning a treatment person to administer the service without the necessary training or experience would be a disservice to both employees and employers.
4. *Evaluation of the EAP service* should be made not on the basis of the number of treatment referrals made, but on other criteria developed as part of the overall business plan. While it is likely that some treatment referrals will be made, it is extremely important that the EAP service operate without obligation to any treatment program, including its own.

Summary

The main point of this chapter is that EAP programs should always be developed with the best interest of employees in mind. When employees do not receive objective assessments of their needs, they may be given an inappropriate referral. As long as EAP providers offer quality services with staff trained to handle a wide range of human problems, affiliation with treatment programs matters little. EAP providers should operate independently from specific treatment programs and should not be evaluated on the number of referrals made to any given program of treatment.

It is also important to remember that what may appear as legitimate concern about conflict of interest may in fact be concern over treatment providers having a perceived unfair advantage in the EAP marketplace. Separation of these issues is critical, and, when in doubt, the true test of conflict of interest should always be applied by asking, "In what ways are employees being disadvantaged by this EAP service?"

As the EAP field changes and new providers of EAP services emerge, we should always protect the interest of our primary clients — employees. A straightforward, open exchange of views is critical to increasing our understanding of controversial issues in our field, and ultimately, in better serving our clients.

The Evolution of the NBC Employee Assistance Program

Morton Aronoff and Henry Huestis

The Early Years

Before 1971, help for troubled employees at NBC was available through the health office under the direction of an understanding company medical director, the late Dr. Bernard Handler. In addition, some recovering alcoholics were doing Twelfth Step work (carrying the A.A. message to others) among co-workers who had alcohol problems. These people were able to assist troubled employees who were willing to open up. Such troubled employees were often in extreme difficulty and had nowhere else to go. But the people being helped represented a small percentage of the problem employee population. The vast majority of employees with problems chose to struggle through, fearful of losing their jobs, of being discovered as alcoholics or other types of drug addicts, or of being labeled as emotional cripples. The stigma connected with personal difficulties was still very much a reality. Covering up the problems was the norm. Well-meaning co-workers, in an effort to "help" fellow workers, compensated for unproductive, troubled employees by doing their work for them rather than reporting work problems to supervisors or shop stewards.

Uninformed and frustrated supervisors spent much of their time trying to correct troubled subordinates' deteriorating job performances. Efforts at scolding, lecturing, pleading, transferring, demoting, and making deals with subordinates met with failures. The union, in seeking to protect its troubled members who were unproductive, filed grievances. Members were encouraged to keep problems of absenteeism, lateness, and unproductivity from management's eyes and ears.

All these factors, combined with more enabling and covering up by family members and the community at large, further contributed to the ultimate downfall of troubled employees at NBC. The final consequences were inescapable. Some employees were terminated. Buy-outs were common. Deals were made by the company and the union. Alcoholics who denied their drug problems resigned their jobs, blamed the company for their problems, and sought geographic cures by finding employment elsewhere. With a generous retirement plan at NBC, some accepted early retirement, believing the Florida sunshine would cure their ills. Others obtained long-term disability. Statistics indicate that those addicted employees who left the job lived an average of eighteen months after leaving. Finally, some employees at NBC suffered death from drug abuse while still working — the tragic result of their illness and others' ignorance, apathy, and misunderstanding. The seeds of the NBC employee assistance program were planted in this environment.

The Alcoholism Assistance Committee

From 1950 through 1971 our efforts to turn the alcoholic employee toward recovery met with almost total failure. Supervisor's threats would, at best, bring about improved performance for one or two months. The alcoholic would abstain for that period or drink only after work. But the alcoholic would inevitably be back on a downward slide.

Two vital elements were missing: 1) the alcoholic employee was not given direction from a program to guide recovery and 2) the company and the union continued their adversarial roles in any confrontation caused by work performance problems.

At NBC in New York, in early 1971, a camera person and an electronic maintenance engineer recruited a third local member from the Telecine (film) studio and formed an Alcoholism Assistance Committee (AAC) with the blessing of the President of Local 11 of the National Association of Broadcast Employees and Technicians (NABET). The members of the AAC had covered up for many alcoholics in the past twenty or more years (one was living with an alcoholic spouse) although they were not alcoholics themselves. They knew the newspaper reports of General Motors and the United Auto Workers collaborating on helping the alcoholic employee on the assembly line were good news for the people in radio and TV broadcasting. Discussions

The EAP Solution

with the New York City Central Labor Council disclosed some evening peer-counseling courses on alcoholism, emotional, family, and marital problems. They started with the substance abuse course and proceeded to learn about this monster — alcoholism — which they had been facing on the job. The course was six weeks long, a total of eighteen hours. Those eighteen hours were the beginning of a pioneer labor-management Occupational Alcoholism Program (OAP) at NBC.

The AAC had approval from the Local President, who was asked to obtain the company's approval to implement a program. It made sense for the company and the union to jointly confront the alcoholic employee with documentation of impaired work performance and to use job security as leverage. The goal was to have the employee admit him- or herself into a Long Island hospital for a seven- to ten-day detoxification, and be introduced to rehabilitation followed by 26 weeks of aftercare. The late Ruth Lassoff, Director of Aftercare in New York City, worked closely with the NABET committee. Ruth was the key person in the treatment phase of our alcoholism program.

The local president asked the Vice President of Personnel if the NABET AAC could start accepting referrals from supervisors and conduct joint confrontations of employees with these supervisors. The immediate response was, "Let's try it."

We were unsure how to proceed. We knew most of the technical managers and directors well. Many had come from the union ranks. The word was spread that a NABET committee was accepting referrals of employees whose job performance had deteriorated (along with a suspicion of excessive use of alcohol).

The committee did receive some referrals — from supervisors, shop stewards, and co-workers. The troubled person was confronted by the supervisor and committee, and for the first time direction for recovery was added to the threats of job jeopardy. The Long Island Hospital program proved to be effective. Although we had only ten referrals in the first twelve months, we were soon aware the program was working. Employees with marginal performance were demonstrating effectiveness and reliability at their jobs. The feedback from supervisors, co-workers, and family members was encouraging.

The New York City Central Labor Council also had a Labor Rehabilitation Committee to take referrals from member unions. We soon found this committee extremely useful as a resource for marital, family, emotional, financial, and other personal problems. However, the AAC continued to exercise control over the assessment and referral process with substance abuse cases. This combination gave NABET Local 11 a broadbrush program in 1971.

Dr. Bernard Handler was a great doctor, human being, and valuable company resource. The NABET committee found an advocate for its program in Dr. Handler. He was our mentor in the early years, helping guide us over the rough spots. For instance, he warned that a program required records, and we instituted a system to follow the progress of the alcoholism referrals. We soon understood the necessity behind his advice and followed it up with a statistical report.

Although our program operated without any written agreement between NBC and NABET Local 11 and without any written sanction from the Executive Board of the local, it was not unique, since at that time the beginnings of many programs were informal. A substantial number of flourishing, successful programs were the result of committed members of A.A. working on their Twelfth Step in the work setting.

Two committees with overlapping memberships evolved: the Alcoholism Assistance Committee (AAC) and the Community Services Committee (CSC). The Member Assistance Program (MAP) was thus established. The CSC was responsible for all nonalcohol-related referrals. Each committee received between ten and fifteen referrals each year from the union ranks. In addition, we received a small number of referrals from nonrepresented employees who knew of our program or were referred by a supervisor who did.

The AAC went through changes in leadership during the first two years. Two members transferred to management and new members were recruited. Henry

The EAP Solution

Huestis, a recovering alcoholic, took the chairmanship of the AAC. Mort Aronoff remained as chairperson of the CSC. Both were TV engineers, working the program as part-time volunteers.

In November 1974 the new MAP leadership made advances after completing an intensive educational course called ACCEPT. In those days, the term "broadbrush" was not used, but many EAPs were taking all referrals and giving assistance for a variety of problems. The committee members took advantage of many courses on peer counseling which were sponsored by the Central Labor Council. We attended the Rutgers University Summer School of Alcohol Studies in 1976 and 1977, and that provided us with another intensive learning experience.

The emergence of the Association of Labor-Management Administrators and Consultants on Alcoholism (ALMACA) presented the opportunity for us to share and grow with the new occupation of EAP counselors. The number of programs in the New York metropolitan area was growing, and we had much to learn from each other. We started with ALMACA membership in 1975, attending the national conferences and national forums of the National Council on Alcoholism. We have made several presentations and delivered papers at local, regional, and national ALMACA conferences, NCA National Forums, and one paper in Munich, Germany at the Twenty-eighth International Institute on the Prevention and Treatment of Alcoholism.

Starting in 1975, our program was aided tremendously by two people — the aforementioned Ruth Lassoff and Robert Hurford, Vice President of Labor Relations, now retired. Bob understood our program, witnessed its effectiveness, and gave the program full support. When Bob knew of an employee being shielded by some well-meaning, misguided supervisor, he did not hesitate to intervene and move the referral to the union program. Our success rate, based on the standard of improved work performance, was over 90 percent. The efforts of both committees gave us visibility and credibility.

The next step, in 1976, was to develop a written policy that would be endorsed by the local's Executive Board. The Executive Board did approve, after much deliberation, that "where all attempts at rehabilitation have failed, termination of employment shall be handled in a consistent and equitable manner — through normal labor relations channels." Our program had reached maturity. Two years later this policy was rewritten and approved in broadbrush language.

Movement Toward a Companywide Program

A campaign to have the program expanded into a much-needed companywide EAP was initiated in 1977. The concept had support from Labor Relations, Personnel, and many executives around the country. NBC has owned and operated stations in New York, Burbank, Chicago, Cleveland, and Washington, D.C. A well-prepared policy was unanimously approved by the top personnel executives at the five stations.

A change in company circumstances brought these moves to a halt. NBC's problems in programming brought about a change in leadership, and the focus changed to programs and ratings. The EAP campaign was shelved, but this did not deter the Local 11 program; we were experiencing positive results. "Constructive coercion" was replaced by "constructive intervention." It was all the same — using evidence of impaired or deteriorating work performance to crack denial and motivate the troubled employee to accept the recommendations of the MAP. It worked well because the last claim to health of the problem employee — the regular job and paycheck — had been jeopardized. When the intervention was jointly held — union and supervisor together confronting the employee — the result was cooperation.

We had looked forward to amassing sufficient alcoholism referrals to warrant a statistical report. We did this in 1977 with 44 referrals and then followed up each year. We continued with a success rate greater than 90 percent, and our program accrued credibility and visibility.

Our persistent efforts to move up to a companywide program were stymied. Requests for meetings with the

The EAP Solution

top personnel executive were not answered. While many of the division heads knew of the work of the union committees, we knew we would need the approval of the Personnel Department and the backing of Labor Relations. We would have to be patient and count our blessings.

The EAP had a real opportunity for change in late 1981 after Grant Tinker became NBC's Chief Executive Officer and Chairperson of the Board. At NBC's annual December reception for 25-year employees, we were introduced to Grant Tinker, who asked us to call his secretary. She understood the importance of the EAP, and scheduled the meeting in February when Tinker would be finished with programming priorities. At the conclusion of that meeting, Tinker turned to us and asked for a proposal. Two months later we gave him our formal proposal titled *An Employee Assistance Program for NBC: The Need, the Benefits, the Structure, the Cost.*

The proposal was prepared with help from many others. We sent preliminary drafts to executives for comments. A lawyer reshaped the final draft for greater clarity and emphasis. After eleven more months and a change in personnel leadership, the proposal became a reality. In March the proposal was accepted by the Executive Vice President, Personnel, and Labor Relations, and we assumed EAP specialist staff positions. Grant Tinker wrote a letter announcing the EAP as of March 28, 1983, and sent it to all employees.

The NBC EAP

It was decided to place the new program in Personnel, reporting to the Vice President of Human Resources. The NABET Local 11 President appointed new committee chairpersons and the MAP remained intact, which made it possible for the EAP and the MAP to work jointly in cases involving union referrals. The EAP office is located in the New York Health Office. It is a confidential area and enabled the EAP to work closely with the company nurses and physician. The two-person staff would be responsible for assisting employees at all locations of NBC. This included the 4,300 employees in New York, which is corporate headquarters, and four other stations owned and operated by

NBC. Also included were NBC's 21 domestic and foreign news bureaus and the San Francisco AM and FM radio stations. The total NBC population was 8,300. The NBC Employee Assistance Program had its maximum impact in New York. Referrals from the other locations were handled mostly by telephone with the help of the ALMACA directory, an invaluable networking resource. The goal of having an EAP set up at each location was to take some time to achieve.

The first location outside New York to recognize the need for its own program was Chicago. A local EAP provider had already demonstrated an effectiveness with the local union MAP and submitted their proposal to the personnel director, who approved it and sent it on to New York for corporate approval. The contract was signed and the Chicago program began in January 1984. Washington D.C. was next, and another local provider was chosen to operate its program in August 1984. Cleveland quickly followed suit in September. Early in 1985, the Director of Employee Counseling and Development was given corporate responsibility for all NBC employee assistance programs and started addressing two issues — the hiring of an EAP specialist for the Burbank location and assessing the delivery of services in each location to assure all employees were receiving the same quality. It was decided that Burbank, with 1,900 employees, would be served best by an in-house program. An EAP specialist was hired in Burbank in July 1985, and the NBC Employee Assistance Program was now complete. Each location had its own EAP operating independently, reporting to its own personnel executive, locally and functionally to the Director at headquarters in New York.

Formal MAPs are in existence in New York, Burbank, and Chicago with NABET program counselors. The cooperative relationship between these union representatives and the EAP staff has insured the success of the company program.

The Joint Program

The evolution from a union-based program to a companywide EAP enhances the workability of the joint

The EAP Solution

process. There is a high degree of mutual respect and absence of an adversarial position. Any union self-referred member may utilize the services of the company EAP or may choose to see the union MAP with complete confidentiality. The MAP and the EAP confer on needs of the employee and appropriate resources. Names are not given without the approval of the troubled employee.

Supervisory referrals are handled differently. If the supervisor contacts the EAP to discuss a possible referral based on work performance issues, the MAP will be contacted. The MAP will be involved in cases where disciplinary action is indicated. A preliminary meeting is held, and a plan of action is developed and implemented by the supervisor and the joint EAP/MAP. If adequate documentation of deteriorating work performance is cited by the supervisor, an intervention is scheduled with the troubled union employee. It is recommended that the MAP member be present at the confrontation to fulfill contractual agreements and to provide evidence to the troubled employee that the EAP/MAP is a joint program. EAP staff might suggest being present if a supervisor feels uncomfortable or unsure of the process. The EAP/MAP then makes a joint recommendation concerning treatment for the union employee.

Disciplinary action including suspension without pay may be involved. These actions must be in writing by the supervisor to the employee and must be approved by NBC Labor Relations, Personnel, and the chairperson of the union grievance committee before delivery to the employee. Grievances or arbitration rarely have been filed following such a procedure. The employee decides whether or not to accept treatment. Should the employee refuse to cooperate, work performance must be maintained at adequate levels.

The MAP and EAP have frequent joint, informal meetings to discuss ongoing caseloads and to attend regional and national conferences together. NBC has always made accommodations to MAP members, giving them time off to attend such meetings. MAP members remain volunteers and have regular jobs in their respective departments.

Case Studies

To aid supervisors using the EAP, NBC has included a segment "Handling Personal Problems" in its management development program called *Effective Management Practices*. This program is conducted by NBC's professional training staff. An EAP staff member is invited to discuss the EAP process and explain how supervisors can use the program. Groups of supervisors including managers, directors, and vice presidents have been participating in these sessions. An NBC-produced videotape demonstrates a supervisory intervention, and an *EAP Supervisor's Guide*, which includes a ten-step program, is distributed to attendees.

Elements the NABET Local 11's MAP Lacked (1971-1982)

Some of the elements that the NABET Local 11's program lacked were

1. *Adequate Staffing:* Since the MAP counselors were employed and paid as engineers, it was only possible to give a portion of their time to handling personal problem referrals. Company business and especially broadcast operations necessarily took top priority.
2. *Supervisor and Shop Steward Training:* Without a formal company EAP and with time constraints of MAP counselors, training became a one-on-one experience, often in hallways or supervisor's offices. Without any official company policy, supervisors could not receive any formal training.
3. *Outpatient Mental Health Coverage:* This was a defect in the previous medical benefits plan. Reimbursement for payment of outpatient mental health care consisted of ten dollars per visit, unchanged over twenty years. Coverage improved with a new benefits plan which pays for a substantial portion of thirty visits over a calendar year. Outpatient chemical dependency treatment programs are now covered.
4. *Malpractice Insurance:* The EAP staff is now eligible under company blanket malpractice insurance.
5. *Formal Written Policy:* During the early and middle stage in the development of the MAP, no written policy existed. A written union policy was issued in

1976, and declared joint management/union efforts were needed. The company accepted this philosophy in practice. The March 1983 letter by Grant Tinker to all NBC employees serves as a policy statement for the companywide EAP.

6. *CEO and Upper Management Support:* Some support was evident throughout the history of the MAP, but not at the CEO level. The CEO support of the EAP was acknowledged formally in the 1983 letter. Grant Tinker and selected executives have met with the EAP staff semiannually since its inception.

7. *Formal Location:* During the time that the MAP functioned, meetings took place in operating areas of the company or the union office, and assessments and referrals were made wherever space could be found. This hampered the program, and confidentiality was difficult to maintain. The New York EAP now operates in the Health Office, and confidentiality is safeguarded. The EAP staff in New York can easily be reached; the 24-hour NBC phone extension in New York is H-E-L-P. Files and confidential records are centrally and securely stored.

Essentials for an Effective Joint Program

The successful joint program will emerge from one or more of a number of causative factors. Some start in union ranks; others spring from management efforts. Many have sprung from recovering alcoholics doing successful Twelve Step work with their co-workers. Executives have pushed for programs after their own recoveries, or after experiencing the frustration of dealing with a high-ranking alcoholic in the organization, or after seeing a close friend or family member succumb to the disease. There were 300 programs nationwide in 1971, and over 8,000 in 1986. Almost all were implemented to help troubled employees; very few, if any, were put in place because of a cost-benefit analysis.

There are some requirements for successful joint EAPs that are constants and cannot be compromised. We have compiled a list of thirteen essentials.

Case Studies

1. *Confidentiality:* Maintenance of confidentiality is a cornerstone of the occupational program. Let it be known that an interaction with the EAP can get back to a supervisor or another department in the organization and the referral rate will rapidly approach zero.
2. *Honesty:* Dealing with the dynamics of denial demands total honesty. The workplace counselor must be open and candid with clients in order to generate trust and honesty in return.
3. *Minimization of Cover-up:* The most destructive force in dealing with severe personal problems in the company is cover-up. Cover-up is the result of ignorance and stigma, and the antidote is education and more education. Well-meaning supervisors, shop stewards, and co-workers must learn that cover-up kills.
4. *Top Union Support:* If there are represented employees in the organization, the adversarial posture will be avoided by getting the support of the union leadership, specifically the union local president, grievance chairperson, and the executive board.
5. *Labor Relations Support:* The correlator to top union support is support from the Labor Relations Department. The labor relations lawyers are happy to see grievances and arbitrations avoided.
6. *Middle Management Support:* Supervisor referrals usually come from middle management. It is vital that they understand the joint EAP process and are willing to use it.
7. *Top Management Support:* For a joint program to be fully functional, top management support is necessary. This support can overcome problems which arise from lack of knowledge and prejudice at lower levels in the organization.
8. *Record Keeping:* We use a daily log which winds up in a computerized data base for easy retrieval. This capability has proven effective and necessary for reporting follow-up and evaluation.

The EAP Solution

9. *Knowledge of EAP Process:* Knowledge and understanding of the EAP process is fundamental. A joint program is not the equivalent of "Twelve Stepping." No element of the procedure can be eliminated without jeopardizing the outcome.
10. *Availability of Appropriate Resources:* Referrals need many types of quality appropriate resources such as public agencies, private agencies, detoxification, rehabilitation, one-on-one therapy, and group therapy. Care required for individual recovery programs include inpatient, outpatient, freestanding, hospital-based, and self-help groups. Most resources must be near the client's community. Long-term inpatient programs can be used anywhere in the United States.
11. *Network of Mentors:* EAP practitioners need ongoing support from many directions — management, union, and other professionals. The EAP counselor also functions best, and avoids burnout, if a network of mentors exists to help with difficult clinical or organizational questions.
12. *Self-Help Groups:* In cases involving chemical dependency or other compulsive behaviors, the strongest support for recovery is in the many self-help groups. A.A., Al-Anon, N.A., C.A., D.A., O.A., and G.A. groups offer a new way of living. People are shown how to achieve abstinence and that abstinence can be continued "one day at a time."
13. *Burnout:* The EAP specialist must be alert to signs of burnout. Some corrective or preventive measures are the following: consult regularly with mentors; utilize professional EAP networks; organize burnout meetings; avoid giving out your home phone number; take periodic vacations; if pressure doesn't ease, consult a therapist; and, above all, TAKE YOUR LUNCH HOUR.

Conclusion

Through this case study, we have shown how an idea to help fellow employees in need grew into an informal union program. This evolved into a formal MAP and,

Case Studies

finally, a companywide EAP. It took patience, perseverance, time, and a lot of help from both management and labor.

The future of the NBC Employee Assistance Program looks bright. The program has achieved maturity, and there is a feeling of trust between the EAP, the MAPs, and the employee population. Self-referrals are on the rise and account for more than 50 percent of the EAP caseload. With the advent of the computer age, we can now store records in our own PC data base, making a meaningful program evaluation possible. The results of a recent random user survey sent to employees who used the EAP and to supervisors who referred subordinates to the EAP, confirmed the program's overall credibility. At this point, the authors feel confident that the program is built on solid ground. It can grow in the future as long as this joint model is continued.

EAPs: Keeping Step

David Levine, M.S.W.

The field of employee assistance programming has evolved considerably over the past fifteen years. Since it is wise to occasionally pause for reflection and speculation, a brief review of some of the changes in the EAP field today is fitting.

This review is entirely biased and far from exhaustive. The reader is encouraged to consider his or her own perceptions and forecasts. However, the structure of this essay may help others organize the various activities that occur under the name of employee assistance. In my experience, everything that occurs within the context of an EAP can be categorized under the headings of counseling, training, evaluation, and management.

Counseling

Although we have seen changes in the area of counseling in the past fifteen years, counseling remains the primary emphasis of employee assistance programs. Counseling is the product. It is the reason training, evaluation, and management exist — to support the counseling. What has changed is how counseling is offered to clients.

Service delivery has evolved because of the needs and pressures of the marketplace. One major change is the existence of multisite delivery systems. A number of providers contract to deliver services to geographically dispersed populations. In some cases, offices and staff are under the direct employ of the EAP contractor. In other cases, a provider will subcontract for services. Many contracting and in-house programs combine full-time staff with subcontracted service to serve dispersed employee groups. Although both methods have been implemented successfully, subcontracting is vulnerable to some risks. As in any decentralized service network, quality control is more difficult to maintain when subcontractors are used. For instance, contracting with inadequately trained staff, permitting referrals to your own program, and "prescreening" by telephone that discourages personal contacts are examples of potential abuses of a subcontracted arrangement. Clearly defined standards and internal quality assurance mechanisms are required of EAP practitioners to avoid compromising service values.

The most prominent change in the health care delivery scene has been cost containment. While HMOs, PPOs, and IPAs have made their mark, EAPs have also kept pace. The focus of occupational alcohol programs on more comprehensive approaches is well-accepted today. The past few years have seen an expansion from assessment and referral to short-term counseling models. The goal is the same — helping people resolve personal problems. The short-term model allows more control over the direction and duration of health care. Some EAPs are now controlling health costs through activities like precertification, concurrent review, and claims and benefits consultation. These new services are clearly motivated by industry's interest in containing health care expenditures. Although organizations other than EAPs have played, and continue to play, a similar role in managing health care benefits, EAPs are naturally suited to play a gatekeeper role with sensitivity to issues of quality and client choice.

Staffing in EAPs has become more professional. Judging from the hiring requirements of most private sector EAPs, as well as federal requirements for programs, master's degrees are generally a minimum standard. Expertise in addictions has remained a priority in the quality programs. The impact of EAPs on the field of human services has helped educate many to the problems of chemical dependency, codependency, and chemical abuse. Schools of social work, psychology, and other mental health professions do not routinely require familiarity with addictions, but MSWs and similarly trained professionals have found familiarity with alcohol and other drug problems essential for employment in EAPs.

The difficult issue of credentialing EAP practitioners is related to staffing. The torch for credentialing has been carried by numerous parties concerned about standards and quality. The issue has received attention

The EAP Solution

from the recent efforts of ALMACA and EASNA,* and controversy abounds at every turn of the process. The breadth of work that EAPs encompass makes it difficult, perhaps impossible, to establish a meaningful credential that encompasses the great variance of practice. Issues of personal investment and ownership continue to raise emotions and debate. ALMACA's 1985 National Conference evidenced a healthy and heated interchange of ideas on the subject, but a unified direction on the issue of credentialing does not appear at hand. Again, the responsibility falls to individual programs and the peers within them to define the most relevant and meaningful standards of service.

Training

The evolution of the EAP field can certainly be recognized in the area of training. Just when many practitioners could recite "The Dryden File" almost verbatim, a wealth of improved training aids hit the market. A great range of EAP training is apparent in the shift from training designed to help supervisors identify and refer problem employees, to more comprehensive educational programs on health-risk appraisal and prevention. Where at one time the purpose of EAP training was to identify and facilitate the treatment of alcoholism, today we see training playing a primary role in not only promoting the direct counseling services of an EAP, but also in educating employees about various health hazards and avoiding health risks. Health educators have taken this prevention approach for years, and in conjunction with an EAP, it is a well-suited educational approach for employees. A good program can determine educational needs through the clinical activities of their counselors, employee surveys, and input from a company's medical and employee relations staff.

---

*The Association of Labor-Management Administrators and Consultants on Alcoholism (ALMACA) and The Employee Assistance Society of North America (EASNA) are the most-established professional associations of EAP practitioners with a national scope.

As a natural complement to EAP counseling, training has seen marked advance. Some of the recent training developments have included health risk appraisals and individual follow-up focusing on problems of hypertension, smoking, chemical abuse, and stress. Other advances can be recognized in response to companywide issues such as organizational change, time management, relocation, expatriation/repatriation, and career adjustment. For example, in some of the depressed steel industries which have had large-scale layoffs, the EAP staffs have become career training and development specialists in response to the changing needs of their organizations. Training has also kept pace with various social problems such as single parenting, day-care, two-career families, AIDS education, and other relevant issues.

Evaluation

Foot and Erfurte, Googins, Roman, Spicer, Owen, Jones, and Trice are but a few of the people who have contributed much to the area of evaluation of EAPs. Not only have these researchers made headway in demonstrating the value of EAPs, but more importantly they have taught practitioners about the need for accountability and how to go about measuring the impact of EAPs. From the early studies of Kennecott Copper employees to more recent cost-benefit projects at General Motors, Health and Human Services, United Airlines, and other companies, most research attests to the efficacy of EAPs. These major research undertakings have helped educate others in the role of evaluation in an EAP. Methodology and sampling procedures have become increasingly rigorous, and the validity of EAP evaluation continues to improve.

In today's EAPs it is rare that some system of measurement is not in place. Measures of effectiveness, such as impact studies on absenteeism and health costs, continue to play an important role. However, many have learned that measures such as program utilization, percent of family involvement, presented versus assessed problems, and referral acceptance rate continue to hold the most relevance for EAP practitioners. When

The EAP Solution

attention is given to measures like these, the feedback can be received in a timely manner and help direct program modifications.

In spite of relative agreement on the measures to monitor, there remains great diversity about how those measures are calculated. Until more consistency in statistical measurement is available, comparisons of various program performance indicators will be difficult and, consequently, so will widely held program standards. Some EAPs with large enough client populations and data bases can attempt to define benchmarks for program performance. But because of the proprietary nature of many programs and corporate confidentiality, standards are not quickly forthcoming. In spite of these realities, some progress has been evidenced through EAP conference presentations and research publications. Evolution toward improved levels of evaluation is apparent.

Computerization has advanced data collection, reporting, and information sharing. Information system programs are available, and their promotion has increased the awareness and sophistication of evaluation in the field. Evaluation will play an increasingly important role as more attention is paid to the cost of an operation, ROI, and various EAP cost-containment service models. As more EAPs become involved in assisting employers to manage their employees' health care benefits, there will be more reliance on numbers and the technology that help provide data.

Management

Few practitioners are left feuding over which model of EAP is better, in-house or contracting. It is clear that in-house programs hold advantages of organizational sensitivity and responsiveness, and contracting programs have an easier time promoting confidentiality. The choice depends on the needs and nature of the employee population. External contractors are providing services to an increasingly larger proportion of programs. This trend will continue, and hybrid programs combining in-house and contracted service (like Exxon, Honeywell, and others) will also become more common.

Case Studies

As EAPS have grown to serve increasingly larger employee populations, our management struggles have become similar to those of other businesses. For instance, the subjects of marketing, organizational stress and change, computerization, quality assurance and supervision, field service delivery, accounting systems, and cash flow are issues that have relevance to many work organizations, including EAPs.

Because of our service orientation, we risk becoming overly isolated in our helping roles. We need to recognize our management struggles for what they are and call on consultants when we need help. Contemporary management gurus encourage increased attention to human resources; participative, decentralized organizational hierarchies; emphasis on individual potential; and reliance on teamwork and cooperation. The people who comprise EAPs surely need to be as mindful of good management practice in their own work groups as they are with the managers they coach.

One of the biggest factors confronting EAPs today relates to the challenge of the future. Because EAPs are positioned to play a key role in changing health care delivery, we hold some control over our destiny. Until recently, our purpose has been to identify health problems and resolve them. We have consulted with benefits people and rallied against sparse HMO plans, but our own economic viability has not been directly related to the cost of health care.

Today that is changing. Because of our role as gatekeeper to health care services, we are expected to assist employers in managing their health care dollars. In some cases, we consider sharing in the risks and profits. We need to be careful. When our own paycheck depends on the cost of health care and how much service is delivered, we may well lose our objectivity. As well-intentioned and ethical as we might be in assuming that role, we cannot avoid being impacted by the cost ceilings of the health care dollars we are managing. As other health care delivery models have demonstrated, economic abuses exist on two sides. Costs escalate unreasonably when there are few checks or balances on how much service is delivered. Abuses also occur when health care access is thwarted in favor of short-term profits. In most cases these delivery systems are full of ethical and well-intentioned providers.

Conclusion

EAPs will continue to evolve and adapt to the changes in health care and industry. The greatest challenges before us are to pursue only those opportunities appropriate to our skills and standards and to preserve our professional values regarding problem identification and service delivery. We can continue to play a powerful role and have an impact on health care, but we need to be creative about how our future business relationships are established and managed.

7
FUTURE ISSUES AND TRENDS

Jerry Spicer, M.H.A.

Licensing and Standards

The development of program standards and certification or licensing requirements for EAP counselors is an issue for the professional associations representing the employee assistance practitioner. It is neither appropriate nor my intention to give a "Hazelden perspective." But those of us delivering EAP services should become well versed in the advantages and disadvantages of standards and look for opportunities to discuss these issues. One of the major obstacles to developing uniform standards is the diversity of models and services within the umbrella concept of employee assistance. EAP practitioners require more than counseling skills, and are often also trainers and consultants. The programs themselves vary from a focus on alcoholism to a broad philosophy of prevention and health promotion. Also, those of us working in the EAP field typically

The EAP Solution

have other professional memberships in chemical dependency, social work, or mental health associations. Whether employee assistance becomes a separate discipline or a speciality within a larger association (or both) will be a significant decision for the future. As professionals, we should be involved whenever possible in developing standards that have a clear and measurable impact on program or client outcome. Until standards are available for the field, we should adhere to the standards of existing professional associations and develop our own internal guidelines for professional conduct.

Drug Testing

Drug testing in the workplace is becoming more common, and employee assistance professionals will need to determine their personal and professional position on testing. A universal standard is not practical as each workplace will have different needs and problems, but an EAP will need to have a clear philosophy and policy on its involvement with drug testing. Some of the facts and issues about drug testing are outlined below.

1. Testing is increasing as more employers test job applicants and current employees. Employers having public safety responsibilities (e.g., air traffic control, transportation industries) are most likely to test employees.

2. The legal issues about drug testing are not fully resolved. Future court decisions will help clarify some of the confusion, but we should expect legal requirements to vary by type of employer (public or private); method and frequency of testing (random vs. all employees, blood or urine tests); background or position of the employee being tested (job applicant or permanent employee, employees previously treated for chemical dependency); and type of drug (especially whether legal or illegal).

3. No test is 100 percent reliable. Error rates vary by laboratory, and false-negative rates (not finding a drug) are higher than false-positive rates (finding a drug that was not present) which can be as high as fifteen percent (Hansen, et al., 1985). Also, error

Future Issues and Trends

rates vary by type of drug. Repeated testings using different laboratory methods are important as a reliability check.
4. A positive test, when confirmed, only indicates use, but not addiction or dependency, nor how recently the drug was used. And therefore, a positive test may not be evidenced in immediate job performance problems.

Advocates of drug testing cite several benefits to testing.
1. Testing can be a way of identifying people who need help and might otherwise go undetected.
2. Employers may have little choice but to use drug testing when public safety or liability factors are present.
3. Testing demonstrates to employees and the public that the employer is serious about the problem.
4. The use of illegal drugs is a legitimate concern for employers, and testing is one way of reducing this problem in the workplace.
5. Testing, particularly when it is random, will act as a deterrent since employees will not know when they are about to be tested and will refrain from using drugs (Masi and O'Brien, 1985).

Opponents of drug testing counter with other issues.
1. Testing can create a "false security" when employers mistakenly assume that testing will solve their drug problems (*US Journal*, 1985).
2. The administration of the tests is too often done in a nonrandom and discriminating manner.
3. Testing creates an atmosphere of distrust between management, employees, and the EAP.
4. Drug testing is unconstitutional.

Given this controversy, the employee assistance practitioner cannot and should not avoid taking a position on testing and working with employers to develop appropriate policies. No doubt some EAPs will venture into the drug testing business while others refuse to be associated with any company using drug tests. However, there are options that allow the EAP to maintain its role of a confidential, helping resource amidst these debates, and this requires the EAP to have a clear philosophical position and understanding of the issues and methods of drug testing. There may be few advantages and many disadvantages for the EAP to be directly involved in testing, but a legitimate opportunity exists for the EAP to be involved in how the employer responds to the test results. Most importantly, the EAP can work with the employer to develop a broader range of intervention, education, and counseling services that focus on the "underlying goal of an EAP . . . to get rid of the problem and not the employee" (Masi and O'Brien, 1986: 32).

Employee Assistance Programs, Alternative Delivery Systems, and Cost Containment

The EAP counselor has always been involved in employee medical benefits, as an interpreter of benefit plans for employees needing further help and often as a consultant in design and policy development. Rising health care costs and changing consumer and business attitudes have resulted in a bewildering array of cost-containment strategies, increased competition, and the development of new or alternate delivery systems. Both internal and external EAPs have responded to this new environment by promoting the cost benefit of their services. The evidence is that an EAP can save an employer money by improving the productivity and health of employees (see Chapter Six). However, there may be a need for the EAP of the future to take a more active role in cost containment. There are professional issues to consider about the appropriateness of a care giver being involved in cost containment. But this section is not necessarily written to persuade EAP practitioners to become more involved, but rather to discuss the trends and possible responses. To control and help manage health care costs, whether for chemical dependency or mental health services, the EAP must be able to 1) control client movement through utilization review and case management procedures — more than referral is required, 2) be capable of working with benefit managers to design policies that provide incentives to

Future Issues and Trends

encourage employee use of cost-effective resources, 3) have a good grasp of the new technologies — PPAs, HMOs, UCR standards, and 4) be able to develop reporting systems to help manage the emerging, complex forms of service.

Figure 16 is a representation of an actual EAP contract. The company is self-insured for half of its employees, paying its own claims but contracting for utilization and precertification from an external agent. The other half of the employees have chosen one of six HMOs offered by the employer. Each HMO has its own screening system to control utilization of services, with emphasis given to lower cost and ambulatory care. The company also has a health promotion program that is perceived as both an employee benefit and a cost-beneficial program. In the midst of this is an external EAP. If the figure is confusing, imagine the complexities facing all of the parties involved! Clearly employees have multiple options and a far-reaching range of services. At the same time, we see the future for many of us in this model — diversity and flexibility — but also a confusing arrangement of unrelated components. Case review, funding, and client flow do not coincide, allowing opportunities for resources to be lost in the system. Add to this the probability of a preferred provider arrangement or some new health maintenance organizations, and the model becomes even more complex.

In all probability, we will soon see the development of new systems which encompass the EAP. Figure 17 gives an example of a preferred provider system where health insurance benefits provide incentives for employees to use the EAP and preferred providers for chemical dependency, mental health, wellness, and other services. In this model the EAP is actively involved in utilization review and the selection and monitoring of preferred providers. Here we see one option for the EAP in the new health care cost-containment scene, but other options also exist. The EAP is well positioned to link the treatment and the business communities. Because of experience in both worlds, the EAP practitioner can take an active role in bringing providers and employers together to develop cost-effective *and* high-quality

192

The EAP Solution

**Figure 16
EAP Model — Current Contract**

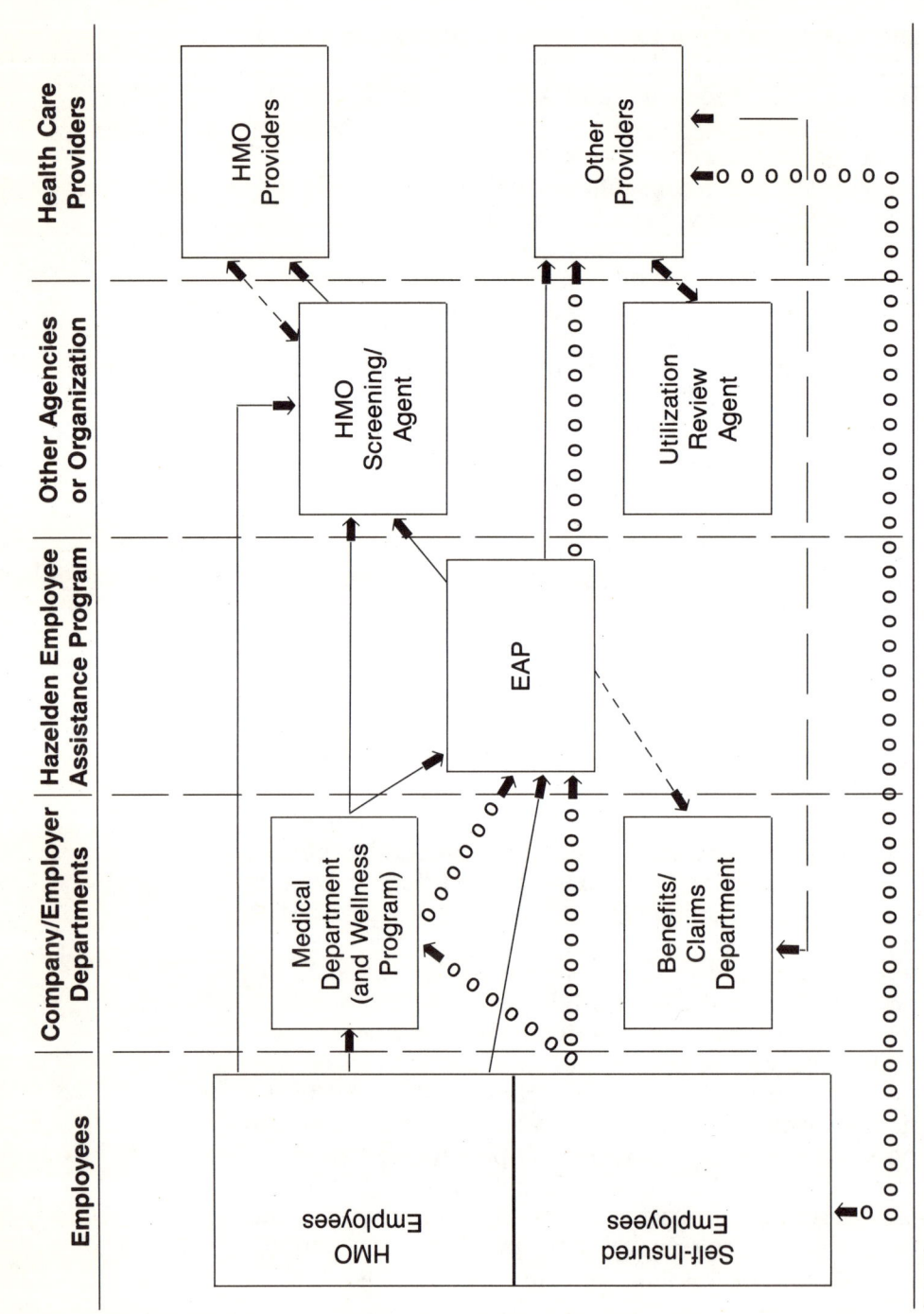

Legend:
Solid line = client flow for HMO employees
Broken line = claims/reimbursement flow
Dotted line = utilization review
Circle line = client flow for self-insured employees

Future Issues and Trends

service delivery systems. The EAP can help select and monitor service quality, costs, and effectiveness to help employers maximize the impact of their health care expenditures. And the EAP can help remind decision makers of the need to strive for long-term outcomes rather than only short-term savings. An example of this commitment to the long-term is in the growing support for wellness or health promotion services, which is discussed next.

Figure 17
Model — EAP Preferred Provider Services

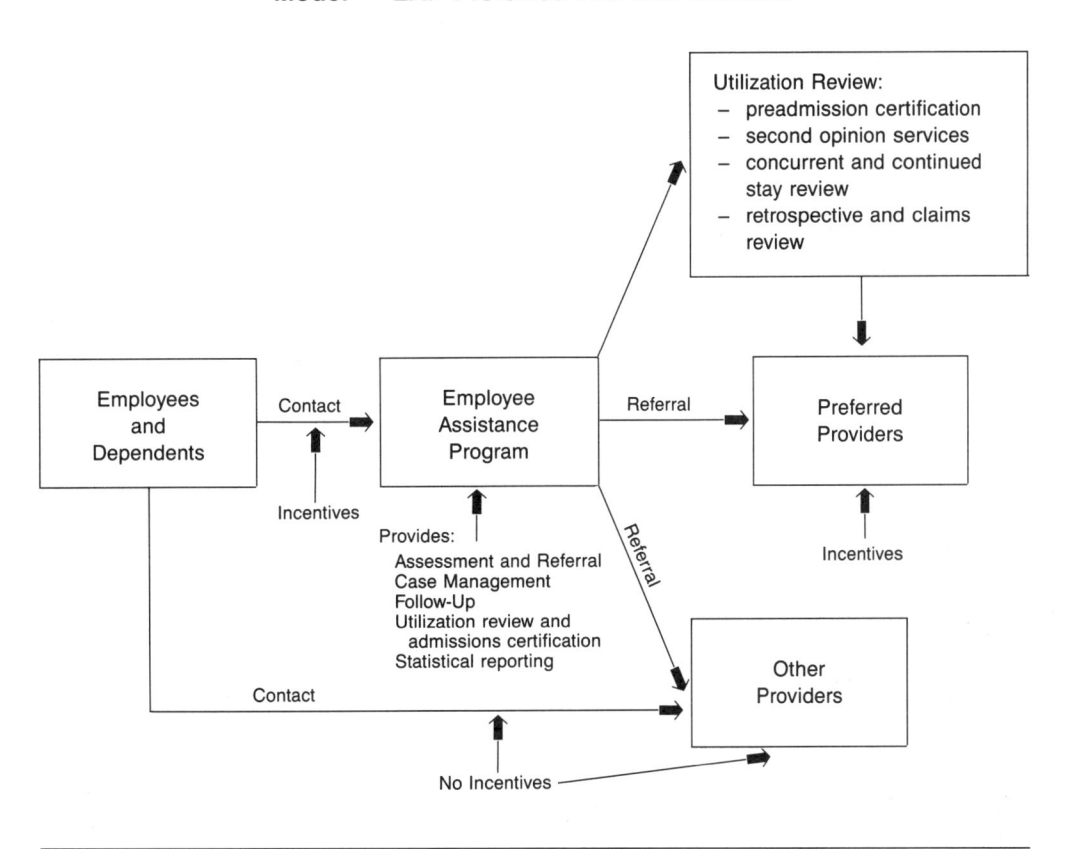

The EAP Solution

HEALTH PROMOTION IN THE WORKPLACE
Thomas Griffin, M.S.W.

Thomas Griffin is the manager of Hazelden's Health Promotion department. These services include occupational programs, adolescent and student assistance services, and Hazelden's newest effort, the Hazelden-CORK Sports Education Program. His background includes several years in alcohol and other drug education. He has authored many articles and books on health promotion, and has a master's degree in social work.

Introduction

The workplace is becoming an increasingly attractive and effective location for the delivery of health promotion services. Employers and employees are beginning to recognize the benefits of designing and developing programs that can improve the health of employees and the organization. For some time, employers have understood that employee assistance services respond to existing employee problems and concerns in an effective manner and can contribute to increased productivity and reduced costs. A recent survey of CEOs of major U.S. corporations reports that over 90 percent of the respondents believe health promotion programs can help control health care costs (Mercer-Meidinger, 1985). A review of popular magazines and newspapers demonstrates a growing interest among the general public for health education through the workplace. Self-help suggestions, advice columns, articles in business sections of daily newspapers, and feature articles on employee health benefits all give testimony to growing interest in the topic.

Parkinson and Associates (1982), have identified the workplace as an ideal environment for a health promotion program. They note that the work site offers

- access to a large number of people
- social support networks to assist employees in improving their lifestyles

Future Issues and Trends

- opportunities for an organization's health professionals to become an integral part of the program
- a focal point for raising the level of health of an entire community

Thus, health promotion programs in the workplace can improve the health of individual employees and the organization's overall productivity. Health promotion programs increase employee's health consciousness, support health-enhancing behaviors, reduce health problems, reduce health care costs, and create a healthier community environment.

The cost-benefit analysis of these efforts is currently underway, and increasingly sophisticated studies are being conducted to quantify the benefits of health promotion programs. These studies will measure both direct cost savings resulting from lower health care costs and reduced absenteeism, as well as indirect productivity benefits resulting from improved morale, high energy levels, and better personal relationships. The research to date indicates the likelihood that cost-effective risk reduction and health promotion programs can be designed and implemented in a variety of work settings.

Assessment of Need

To design and develop effective health promotion efforts, it is necessary to assess the specific needs and resources of an organization. Some programs fail to grasp the attention of employees or the support of management because the unique value of the program to their company is never identified.

A first step in developing an effective program is to assess the specific needs of the organization. There are a number of methods to determine these needs.

1. *Review of Health Care Claims:* Each company has a unique experience in responding to the health needs of its employees. Careful review of recent health care claims can identify the most significant health care problems and costs within the organization.
2. *Employee Attitude and/or Interest Survey:* A well-constructed survey of a representative sample of employees can provide program planners with helpful

The EAP Solution

Figure 18
Health Promotion Model

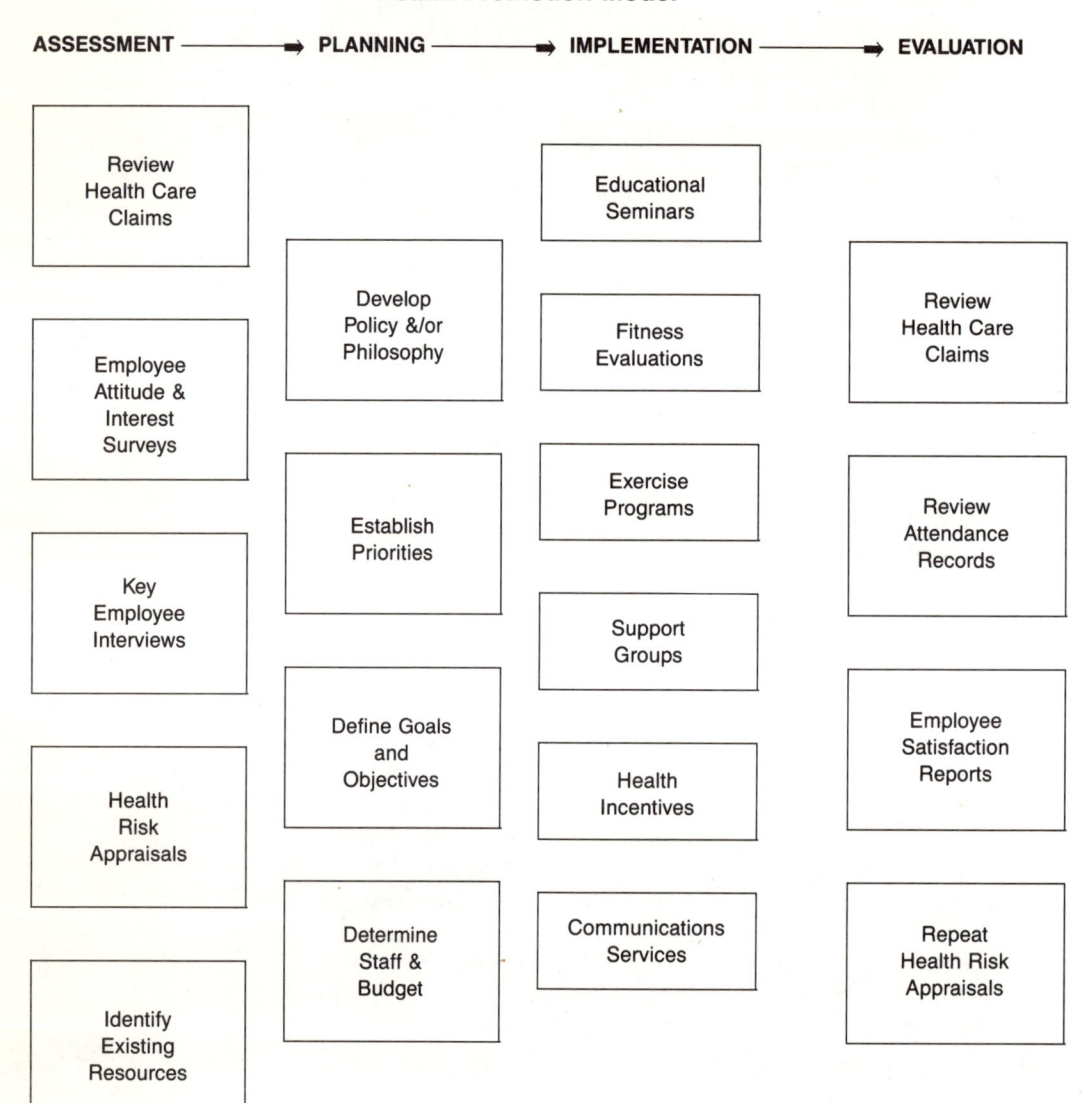

ASSESSMENT → PLANNING → IMPLEMENTATION → EVALUATION

ASSESSMENT	PLANNING	IMPLEMENTATION	EVALUATION
Review Health Care Claims		Educational Seminars	
	Develop Policy &/or Philosophy	Fitness Evaluations	Review Health Care Claims
Employee Attitude & Interest Surveys			
	Establish Priorities	Exercise Programs	Review Attendance Records
Key Employee Interviews		Support Groups	
	Define Goals and Objectives	Health Incentives	Employee Satisfaction Reports
Health Risk Appraisals			
	Determine Staff & Budget	Communications Services	Repeat Health Risk Appraisals
Identify Existing Resources			

information regarding employees' perceptions of health problems and health promotion efforts. A survey can provide direction for program development and can increase the likelihood of employee participation.
3. *Key Employee Interviews:* Structured interviews with selected representatives from all levels and departments within an organization can provide additional information about employee interest, attitudes, and values concerning health. These interviews also serve the purpose of increasing employee involvement in program implementation by designing programs to meet the specific needs of staff.
4. *Health Risk Appraisals:* Aggregate data from health risk appraisals completed by employees can provide specific data on immediate health risks and suggest appropriate health risk behaviors that should be addressed by the health promotion program. Priorities can be identified by analyzing the aggregate data and determining immediate and long-term risk to the work force.

Each of these assessment strategies can be helpful in identifying needs and should be considered complementary to each other. While assessing need, it is also helpful to review current policies, procedures, staff, and other resources relevant to health promotion services. Often, existing services may be in place and must be integrated into any newly designed effort. In addition, underutilized resources may be identified and expanded in emerging efforts.

Planning

After collecting and analyzing assessment information, program planners must identify priorities for the organization and establish goals and objectives relevant to their unique characteristics. Programs that fail to establish priorities and goals can quickly discover employees are not satisfied with current efforts and that it is difficult to measure program effectiveness. Specific planning strategies can include:

The EAP Solution

1. *Development of Policy or Philosophy Statement:* To provide direction to staff developing strategies and services, an administration or board position statement is helpful to provide direction, incentive, and encouragement. A clear rationale for health promotion efforts can also serve as a boost to employee morale since, by its nature, the statement will support the value and contribution of the individual employee.
2. *Establish Program Priorities:* Based on an analysis of the health care claims, health risk appraisals, and employee attitudes and interests, a set of priorities should be identified. Specific health problems and associated risk factors can be compared to employee interests, and priorities can be established.
3. *Define Program Goals and Objectives:* Emerging from this priority list, specific goals and measurable objectives must be articulated. Translating needs assessment information into objectives will insure program efforts are relevant to the organization, are achievable, and are likely to have the desired effect of reducing health risks and improving employee health.
4. *Determine Budget and Staff Needs:* A critical factor in translating goals and objectives into action are the human and financial resources available for the program. Some strategies require little money and staff support, others require sophisticated equipment and professional staffing. Budget and staff decisions must reflect the goals of the program and the fiscal reality of the company. Some organizations have planned for a slow growth for health promotion efforts while others have invested significant resources to initiate programs. At this phase, care must be taken to recognize both short-term and long-term program benefits.

Whether organizations rely on voluntary health organizations for support of low-budget programs or invest large amounts of capital in a health promotion facility, the planning of the program must insure that the efforts are relevant to the needs and interests of both employees and the organization.

Future Issues and Trends

Program Implementation

Program implementation can be designed to reflect needs and interests of both employer and employees. Given the physical and financial resources available, a variety of strategies can be employed to meet program goals and objectives. Specific strategies can include

1. *Educational Seminars*

   A basic component in most health promotion programs is educational sessions designed to provide employees with information about specific health topics as well as an opportunity to talk with colleagues and instructors about ways to apply that information to daily living. Educational seminars can range from informal bag lunch discussions to regularly scheduled classes on relevant health issues. Employers may schedule specific programs for all members of a department or offer programs on a voluntary and optional basis.

2. *Fitness Evaluations*

   Often, people equate health promotion programs with exercise. Physical fitness is a common goal of many people, yet it is difficult to achieve. A first step in the process for most adults is a fitness evaluation designed to determine current levels of fitness and readiness to begin an extensive program of regular exercise. The fitness evaluation can be conducted by a person with training and expertise in exercise physiology. This experience better enables participants to initiate efforts that are likely to reduce health risks and enhance current health conditions.

3. *Exercise Programs*

   There are many opportunities for employers to offer exercise programs even without a fully equipped recreation center. Aerobic exercise and dance sessions can be conducted in large conference rooms if showers are accessible. Financial support for membership and participation in community exercise programs is another option. Small areas can provide space for exercycles and other exercise machines. Regardless of where programs are conducted, regular exercise has been consistently shown to provide positive health benefits including increased cardiovascular stress reduction and weight control.

4. *Support Groups*
The dramatic increase in self-help groups in the past decade indicates their value for persons working to live healthy and satisfying lives. Current research on prevention of health behavior problems also indicates the value of peer social support. The workplace can be an effective location for meeting with people sharing similar goals. Alcoholics Anonymous, Overeaters Anonymous, and quit smoking support groups are just a few examples of groups that can be a component of any health promotion effort.

5. *Health Incentives*
Changing behaviors is not easy and may often require an external incentive to encourage a person to make the necessary effort. Cash rebates for achieving or maintaining goals, public recognition for participation or achievement, "health" leave policy rather than sick leave, and prizes or awards for participation can all be used to encourage active participation.

6. *Communication Services*
Regular newsletters announcing current programs, providing new information about health issues, and soliciting employee ideas and participation can serve to improve program effectiveness. Employees are reminded both of opportunities available and of their organization's commitment to the health of its employees. Other communication services can include aggregate information about employee involvement in health promotion programming, cost savings to the organization, and program philosophy and goals.

Program implementation strategies can correspond with organizational and employee goals and interests. Strategies can be packaged to encourage active support and involvement of all staff. Programs can also be structured to allow varying degrees of employee effort and involvement. Implementation strategies should be complementary to each other and relevant to program goals and objectives.

Future Issues and Trends

Evaluation

Ongoing evaluation of program implementation and impact can provide valuable information to program planners to allow refinement and adjustment of future efforts as well as to determine the effectiveness of strategies being used. Some specific examples of evaluation strategies include

1. *Review of Health Care Claims and Employee Records*
   Systematic review of health care claims allows the organization to determine if health promotion efforts seem to be having an impact on type of claims and associated costs. Recent history of health promotion efforts in the workplace indicates the likelihood that health care claims and costs can be positively impacted (Gibbs, 1985). One consistently identified goal of health promotion efforts in the workplace is the reduction of absenteeism. A careful review of attendance records can provide a clear measure of program impact. Some organizations report significant reductions in unscheduled absenteeism associated with health promotion efforts.

2. *Employee Satisfaction Reports*
   As a method of monitoring programs, each participant should be asked to indicate his or her level of satisfaction and understanding of specific services. Employee feedback offers immediate information which can be used to modify, strengthen, or continue programs. Employee satisfaction reports also assure employee input in program design and are likely to keep morale high and increase support for future efforts.

3. *Health Risk Appraisals*
   A repeat of health risk appraisals by employees completing the process in the early phases of program development can provide participating employees with specific information regarding changes in health behavior and corresponding health risks. It can also allow the employer the opportunity to compare aggregate data from all participating employees to determine what behavior changes have occurred. It is important to allow enough time between appraisals to see health behavior changes occur.

The EAP Solution

Health promotion programs in the workplace offer an ideal opportunity to respond to existing problems, prevent future problems from occurring, and promote the health of individual employees as well as the organization. Employee assistance services, health education services, exercise programs, group support opportunities, and regular information about services available, can be integrated in order to improve the health and productivity of the work force.

An organizational philosophy and mission which emphasize the value of human resources is the first step to building an effective system of health services for employees. The next steps can be determined by a process of carefully assessing need; planning relevant goals, objectives, and strategies; implementing practical programs; and evaluating program process and impact.

References

Brennan, M. E., *Containing Corporate Health Care Costs — 1983*, Brookfield, WI, International Foundation of Employee Benefit Plans, 1983.

Diesenhaus, H. I., "Program Standards: Can We Ever Agree?" *Employee Assistance Quarterly*, 1(2): 1-17, 1985/86.

Gibbs, J., "Work-site Health Promotion: Five-year Trend in Employee Health Care Costs," *Medical Benefits*, November: 9-10, 1985.

Hansen, H. J., "Crisis in Drug Testing," *Medical Benefits*, May 4, 1985. (Also see the *Journal of the American Medical Association*, April 26, 1985.)

Joint Standards Committee, "Standards for Employee Alcoholism and/or Employee Assistance Programs," *Labor-Management Alcoholism Journal*, Nov/Dec XI(3): 83-87, 1981.

Legal Action Center, "Urine Testing: Practical and Legal Questions," *Of Substance*, March/April 1984: 1-2.

Masi, D. and M. O'Brien, "Dealing With Drug Abuse in the Workplace," *Business and Health*, 29-32, 1985.

Mercer-Meidinger, *Employer Attitudes Toward the Cost of Health*, New York, NY, William and Mercer-Meidinger, Inc., 1985.

Opatz, J., "Wellness Is a Cost-Containment Strategy," *Medical Benefits*, July 4-5, 1985.

Parkinson, R., *Managing Health Promotion in the Workplace: Guidelines for Implementation and Evaluation*, Palo Alto, CA., Mayfield Publishing, 1982.

U.S. Journal, "Mandatory Urine Screening Creates 'False Security,'" April, 1985.

A Final Note

Employee assistance programs have been successful because of support from employers, the community, employees, and families. The early work of the pioneers who brought a new awareness of alcoholism to the business world has been a solid foundation allowing expansion of the original model to include services for today's problems. Future issues will be to maintain our basic mission of helping the chemically dependent person while developing cost-effective ways to help employees with other problems; to strike a balance between the realities of quality and cost containment; to develop as a profession and resolve potentially divisive conflicts over issues such as internal/external models, conflict of interest, or credentialing; and to maintain the support of employers and employees. New services will be added to the EAP model as changes in health care, business, and employees' lifestyles require attention to cost containment, health promotion, employee productivity, and new health problems.

The future will be a time of continued change and opportunities. When the first referral was made by a recovering employee several decades ago, no thought was given to where the EAP field was going. Today's philosophy should be the same — how we change should reflect the needs of employees and employers.

I opened this book by discussing how the development of employee assistance programs parallels the evolution of the public health movement. Public health efforts had a dramatic and measurable impact on health through the reduction of contagious and childhood diseases. Current public health attention is now focused on lifestyle diseases which are not easily or quickly changed. The employee assistance professional has always understood the complexity of changing health behaviors. Our goals are not easily accomplished. We will be successful if we keep the support and involvement of business, employees, and the community. Hopefully, this book will be of value to those of us who share this common goal.

APPENDIX

Recommended Resources

Written Materials

Hazelden EAP publications
A wide variety of employee assistance program leaflets, pamphlets, and books for both managers and employees is available from Hazelden Educational Materials. Call or write for a free catalog from

> Hazelden Educational Materials
> Box 176, Pleasant Valley Road
> Center City, MN 55012
> (800) 328-9000 Toll Free. U.S. Only.
> (800) 257-0070 Toll Free. Minnesota Only.

Other Professional Publications

"Employee Assistance Quarterly," Haworth Press, 75 Griswold Street, Binghamton, NY 13904.

"EAP Digest," Performance Resource Press, 2145 Crooks Road, Suite 103, Troy, MI 48084.

"Medical Benefits," Kelly Communications, 410 East Water Street, Charlottesville, VA 22901.

"The Almacan," 1800 N. Kent Street, Suite 907, Arlington, VA 22209.

Hazelden Audiovisual Materials

Films and Video Cassettes
Everybody Wins
Your Move
(Available in 16mm film, 3/4" video, 1/2" VHS)

Slide Programs
EAP Training Programs
All available from Hazelden Educational Materials
(800) 328-0500 Toll Free, Film and Video Orders, U.S. Only.

Professional Associations

AFL-CIO Department of Community Services, 815 8th Street N.W., Washington, D.C. 20006.

Alcohol and Drug Problems Association, 444 North Capitol Street, Department E., Washington, D.C. 20005.

Association of Labor-Management Administrators and Consultants on Alcoholism, 1800 North Kent Street, Suite 907, Arlington, VA 22209.

Employee Assistance Society of North America, 2145 Crooks Road, Suite 103, Troy, MI 48084.

National Association of Social Work, Occupational Social Work Task Force, 7981 Eastern Avenue, Silver Springs, MD 20910

National Council on Alcoholism, 733 3rd Avenue, Suite 1405, New York, NY 10017

National Institute on Alcoholism and Alcohol Abuse, Occupational Program Branch, 5600 Fishers Lane, Rockville, MD 20857

Most cities and states also have local ALMACA chapters and employee assistance associations.

Education and Training Opportunities

The organizations listed can be contacted regarding training.

Grantsmanship Center, 1031 South Grand Street, Los Angeles, CA 90015. The Grantsmanship Center provides training on grant and proposal writing.

Hazelden Workshops: Hazelden Continuing Education Department, Box 11, Center City, MN 55012, (800) 464-8844.

1. Developing Employee Assistance Programs. A three-day introductory workshop on the basics of employee assistance programming.
2. Evaluating Employee Assistance Programs. A one-day workshop on EAP research and evaluation.

Appendix

Wilson Learning, 6950 Washington Avenue South, Eden Prairie, MN 55344, (612) 944-2880. Wilson Learning's course on Counselor Selling is directed at health care marketing and sales.

Sample Forms and Data Collection Instruments

Assessment/Referral Form - this form is the basic data collection instrument for Hazelden's EAP management information system (SCORE).

Initial Client Questionnaire - data on this questionnaire is used to document clients presenting problems and service history at the time of first contact with the EAP.

One-Month Follow-Up Interview Questionnaire - mail or telephone interviews are conducted with EAP clients at one-month following referral to assess program impact and satisfaction with services.

Employee Assistance Program Survey - this instrument is used for all employee surveys.

Customer Survey - this questionnaire is regularly sent to company EAP coordinators to assess the contractor's satisfaction with the EAP.

Sample Utilization Report

Sample Policy Statement

The EAP Solution

Figure 19

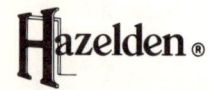

Hazelden® ASSESSMENT/REFERRAL FORM
HAZELDEN EMPLOYEE ASSISTANCE SERVICES

FOR HAZELDEN USE ONLY

| Contract | Client number | Continued Case Management ☐ | Follow-Up Permission ☐ | PPO Client ☐ |

CLIENT INFORMATION

1. Client Name (First Name, Last Name)

   Address (Street or P.O. Box)

   (City) (State) (Zip)

   Work Phone (___) ___-____   Home Phone (___) ___-____

2. Name of Health Insurance

3. Health Insurance Type:
   ☐ HMO   ☐ Other

4. Client Status: ☐ (1) Employee   ☐ (3) Child
                   ☐ (2) Spouse   ☐ (4) Other

5. Client Age: ___   6. Client Sex: ☐ Male ☐ Female

7. Marital Status: ☐ (1) Married   ☐ (3) Divorced/Separated
                    ☐ (2) Single   ☐ (4) Other

8. Client Race: ☐ (1) Caucasian ☐ (3) Black   ☐ (5) Other
                 ☐ (2) Hispanic   ☐ (4) Oriental

EMPLOYEE INFORMATION (FOR ELIGIBLE EMPLOYEE)

9. Employee Name (First Name, Last Name)

10. Employer

11. Employee Division or Unit

12. Company Location (City & State)

13. Job Classification:
    ☐ Supervisor   ☐ Non-supervisor

14. Employee Occupation:

15. Years with Employer: ___

CONTACT INFORMATION

16. Date of first A/R Session:

17. Date of last A/R Session:

18. Referral Source (check one):
    ☐ (1) Self
    ☐ (2) Family member
    ☐ (3) Supervisor-job performance
    ☐ (4) Supervisor-personal concern
    ☐ (5) Hazelden Help Line
    ☐ (6) Union
    ☐ (7) Company representative
    ☐ (8) Other

19. Name of Referring Supervisor:

20. Reason For Contact:
    ☐ (1) Problem assessment
    ☐ (2) Re-assessment (new problem or new referral)
    ☐ (3) Consultation (to refer employee to EAP)

PROBLEM ASSESSMENT

21. Problems Assessed By Counselor (check all that apply):
    ☐ (1) Marital/personal relationships
    ☐ (2) Other family relationships
    ☐ (3) Emotional/mental health
    ☐ (4) Client alcohol use
    ☐ (5) Client other drug use
    ☐ (6) Family alcohol use
    ☐ (7) Family other drug use
    ☐ (8) Legal
    ☐ (9) Financial
    ☐ (10) Job stress
    ☐ (11) Educational/occupational
    ☐ (12) Physical/sexual abuse
    ☐ (13) Other

22. Primary Problem Requiring Referral (1-13): ___

REFERRAL INFORMATION

23. Referral Recommendation (check only one):
    ☐ (1) Client did not complete assessment
    ☐ (2) No referral needed
    ☐ (3) Client refused referral
    ☐ (4) Community resource
    ☐ (5) Community resource-preferred provider
    ☐ (6) Help Line referral to EAS Service Center
    ☐ (7) Short-term EAP counseling

24. Referral Provider Type (check only one for referred clients):
    ☐ (1) Inpatient/hospital treatment
    ☐ (2) Structured outpatient program
    ☐ (3) Individual, family, or group therapy
    ☐ (4) Self-help group
    ☐ (5) Legal counseling
    ☐ (6) Financial counseling
    ☐ (7) HMO
    ☐ (8) Other

PROVIDER INFORMATION (FOR REFERRED CLIENTS)

25. Provider Name (from 24 above):

26. Agency Name (if applicable):

27. Agency Address: (City) (State) (Zip)

28. Provider or Agency Phone: (___) ___-____

EAP SERVICE TRANSACTIONS (FOR ALL CLIENTS)

29. Number of A/R Sessions With Client: ___ In-person sessions ___ Telephone sessions

30. Name of EAP Service Center:

31. City and State:

32. Counselor Name (Print):

EAS-0911   WHITE-Hazelden EAS — YELLOW-File Copy
Copyright © Hazelden Foundation 1986. All rights reserved.

Appendix

Figure 20

Your Name: _____
Date: _____

HAZELDEN
EMPLOYEE ASSISTANCE SERVICES
INITIAL CLIENT QUESTIONNAIRE

This questionnaire is designed to help you indicate in what ways you might want some assistance. Please check the most appropriate response or fill in the answer. *YOUR RESPONSES ARE CONFIDENTIAL.*

Using the scale below, please circle the response which best describes problems you may have in the following areas:

Problems with:	significant problem	some concern	no problem	doesn't apply
1. Raising children?	4	3	2	1
2. Relating to your spouse or significant other?	4	3	2	1
3. Dealing with your own alcohol use?	4	3	2	1
4. Dealing with other drugs (specify_____)?	4	3	2	1
5. Handling job related stress?	4	3	2	1
6. Managing finances?	4	3	2	1
7. Handling legal problems?	4	3	2	1
8. Handling psychological or emotional problems?	4	3	2	1
9. Alcohol or drug problems in family?	4	3	2	1
10. Handling health problems?	4	3	2	1
11. Handling occupational problems?	4	3	2	1
12. Physical or sexual abuse?	4	3	2	1
13. Handling educational problems?	4	3	2	1
14. Other problems? explain_____	4	3	2	1

15. What is the primary problem that has brought you to Employee Assistance Services?
_____
_____

During the past year, have you: YES   NO
16. Used an employee assistance program?   ___   ___
17. Participated in inpatient treatment?   ___   ___
18. Participated in outpatient counseling?   ___   ___
19. Participated in individual therapy?   ___   ___
20. Participated in family therapy?   ___   ___
21. Participated in group therapy?   ___   ___
22. Participated in self-help group therapy?   ___   ___
23. Other... please explain _____

24. Do you feel that your job is in jeopardy at this time?
    ___Yes   explain _____
    ___No

25. In the last month has your job performance:
    ___Improved   ___Stayed the same   ___Gotten worse

26. Who referred you to EAS? _____
27. Has your supervisor ever encouraged you to use EAS? _____

CLIENT TO COMPLETE BEFORE SEEING COUNSELOR

The EAP Solution

Figure 21

Hazelden®
1—MONTH FOLLOW-UP INTERVIEW
HAZELDEN EMPLOYEE ASSISTANCE SERVICES

FOR HAZELDEN USE ONLY	
1. Contract:	2. Hazelden Client No.

3. Date of Contact: ___/___/___
4. Type of Contact: ☐ (1) Telephone
☐ (2) In-Person

5. Client's Name: _____ Home Phone: _____ Work Phone: _____
6. Eligible Employee's Company: _____

FOLLOW-UP CONTACT RECORD

7. Did you contact the referral(s) given to you by your counselor?
   ☐ (1) Yes-which one(s)? _____
   ☐ (2) None were given-why? _____
   ☐ (3) No-explain: _____

If client is covered by an HMO (Health Maintenance Organization), complete this section. If not, proceed to question #11.

8. Did the HMO agree with your counselor's assessment of your problem(s)?
   ☐ (1) Yes
   ☐ (2) No-explain: _____

9. Did the HMO agree with your counselor's recommendation for a referral?
   ☐ (1) Yes
   ☐ (2) No-explain: _____

   If not, what other referral was made? _____

10. Did the HMO pay for the services to which you were referred?
    ☐ (1) Yes
    ☐ (2) No-explain: _____

11. Are you still receiving services from the referral?   ☐ (1) Yes   ☐ (2) No
12. Are you satisfied with the **referral**?
    ☐ (1) Yes
    ☐ (2) No-explain; _____

13. Do you need additional help from the Employee Assistance Program?
    ☐ (1) Yes-explain: _____
    ☐ (2) No

14. Overall, how satisfied are you with the Employee Assistance Program?
    ☐ (1) Very satisfied   ☐ (4) Dissatisfied
    ☐ (2) Satisfied   ☐ (5) Very dissatisfied-explain: _____
    ☐ (3) Neither satisfied nor dissatisfied

15. Do you have any other comments? _____

16. Have you changed your address or phone?   ☐ (1) Yes   ☐ (2) No
    New addresss: _____ New Telephone: _____

Name of Agency:	
City or Town:	State:
Person completing form:	Date:

EVA 918 (9-81) Copyright © Hazelden Foundation 1982. All rights reserved.   **WHITE:** Hazelden EAS   **YELLOW:** File Copy

Appendix

Figure 22

EMPLOYEE ASSISTANCE PROGRAM SURVEY

Would you take a few minutes to give us some information which will help us improve the Employee Assistance Program? All your comments are confidential. Only statistical summaries will be prepared, your individual responses will not be identified. Thank you for your time.

UNDERSTANDING OF THE PROGRAM

These first questions ask about your understanding and familiarity with the Employee Assistance Program.

1. How familiar are you with the Employee Assistance Program? (Check one)
   - ☐ (1) Have never heard of it
   - ☐ (2) Have heard of it, but do not know much about it
   - ☐ (3) Know a little about it
   - ☐ (4) Know a lot about it

Have you: (Check "yes" or "no" for **each** item)

	(1) Yes	(2) No	(3) Not Sure
2. Attended a training or orientation session during which the Employee Assistance Program was explained?	☐	☐	☐
3. Received printed materials mailed to your home that concern the Employee Assistance Program?	☐	☐	☐

4. How do you think we could increase your and other employee's knowledge about the Program? _____
_____
_____

Please answer the following questions based on your understanding of the Employee Assistance Program.

	(1) Yes	(2) No	(3) Not Sure
5. Can members of an employee's family use the program?	☐	☐	☐
6. Do employees have to pay when they initially contact a representative of the Employee Assistance Program?	☐	☐	☐
7. Can employees who have personal problems other than alcohol or drug problems use the Employee Assistance Program?	☐	☐	☐
8. Will the employer be informed when employees contact the Employee Assistance program?	☐	☐	☐
9. Can you use the Employee Assistance Program after work, on weekends, or on holidays?	☐	☐	☐

The EAP Solution

UTILIZATION OF THE PROGRAM

Now we would like to ask you about using the Employee Assistance program.

10. Are there any reasons why you would **not** want to use the Employee Assistance program?
    _____
    _____
    _____
    _____

11. Have you or members of your family ever used the Employee Assistance Program?
    ☐ (1) Yes
    ☐ (2) No one has used the program - **Skip to question 18.**

If you have used the program, how satisfied were you with the following aspects of the program?

	(1) Very satisfied	(2) Satisfied	(3) Indifferent or mildly dissatisfied	(4) Very dissatisfied	(5) Not applicable
12. Accessibility of the Assessment and Referral counselors?	☐	☐	☐	☐	☐
13. Quality of service provided by the Assessment and Referral Counselors?	☐	☐	☐	☐	☐
14. The impact the help provided had on helping you with your problems?	☐	☐	☐	☐	☐
15. The way your confidentiality was protected?	☐	☐	☐	☐	☐

16. How could we improve the services we provided? _____
    _____
    _____
    _____

17. If you have used the Employee Assistance Program, how did your job performance change after contacting the Employee Assistance Program?
    ☐ (1) My job performance improved significantly
    ☐ (2) My job performance improved somewhat
    ☐ (3) My job performance stayed about the same
    ☐ (4) My job performance worsened
    ☐ (5) I'm not sure how my job performance changed

Appendix

INFORMATION ABOUT YOURSELF

Finally we would like some information about you to help us better understand how well the Employee Assistance Program is working.

18. Which of the following best describes your job? (Check only one)
    - ☐ (1) Clerical
    - ☐ (2) Managerial/Supervisory
    - ☐ (3) Sales
    - ☐ (4) Skilled/Trade
    - ☐ (5) Technical/Professional
    - ☐ (6) Other - please explain: _____

19. Which sex are you?
    - ☐ (1) Male   ☐ (2) Female

20. What is your marital status?
    - ☐ (1) Single
    - ☐ (2) Married
    - ☐ (3) Divorced or separated
    - ☐ (4) Widowed

21. How old are you?
    - ☐ (1) Under 25
    - ☐ (2) 25-40
    - ☐ (3) 41-55
    - ☐ (4) Over 55

22. How long have you been with this employer?
    - ☐ (1) Less than one year
    - ☐ (2) At least one year, but less than three years
    - ☐ (3) At least three years, but less than five years
    - ☐ (4) Five years or more

FOR MANAGERS AND SUPERVISORS

If you are a manager or supervisor, please complete this section.

Have you as a manager/supervisor called or used the Employee Assistance Program for any of the following reasons:

	(1) Yes	(2) No
23. To refer an employee?	☐	☐
24. For management consultation?	☐	☐

(Continued on back page)

The EAP Solution

25. If you did refer employees to the Employee Assistance Program how did their job performance improve after contacting the EAP? (Check one)
    - ☐ (1) Performance improved significantly
    - ☐ (2) Performance improved somewhat
    - ☐ (3) Performance stayed about the same
    - ☐ (4) Performance worsened
    - ☐ (5) I'm not sure how performance changed
    - ☐ (6) I have not referred any employees to the EAP

26. Based on your experience with the Employee Assistance Program, how helpful has the program been for you?
    - ☐ (1) Very helpful
    - ☐ (2) Somewhat helpful
    - ☐ (3) Not helpful
    - ☐ (4) I haven't had enough experience with the program to express an opinion

* *

PLEASE ADD ANY ADDITIONAL COMMENTS YOU HAVE ABOUT THE EMPLOYEE ASSISTANCE PROGRAM IN THE SPACE BELOW:

When you have finished, return the questionnaire in the enclosed envelope. No postage is required. Thank you.

Appendix

Figure 23

Hazelden Employee Assistance Services
Customer Survey

Section I - Overall Evaluation

Please check the response you most agree with or fill in your answer.

1. Considering the entire Employee Assistance Program, how satisfied have you been with it?
   - ☐ (1) very satisfied
   - ☐ (2) mostly satisfied
   - ☐ (3) satisfied
   - ☐ (4) indifferent or mildly dissatisfied
   - ☐ (5) not very satisfied

   Comments? _____
   _____
   _____
   _____

2. What have you liked best about your Employee Assistance Program?
   _____
   _____
   _____

3. How could we improve your Employee Assistance Program?
   _____
   _____
   _____
   _____

4. Would you recommend Hazelden to another company interested in an Employee Assistance Program?
   - ☐ (1) yes, definitely
   - ☐ (2) yes, probably
   - ☐ (3) not sure
   - ☐ (4) probably not - why?
     _____
     _____
   - ☐ (5) definitely not - why?
     _____
     _____

The EAP Solution

Section II - Rating of Services

In this section please rate each of the following services on a scale where 1 equals excellent, 2 equals good, 3 equals fair, 4 equals poor, and 5 equals not applicable, or not sure. Also, please add any comments you have on each service area.

Rating:

5. The initial visits and presentation by EAP staff.. _____
   Comments: _____
   _____

6. Employee orientations.. _____
   Comments: _____
   _____

7. Supervisory trainings.. _____
   Comments: _____
   _____

8. Written materials.. _____
   Comments: _____
   _____

9. Our prices and fees.. _____
   Comments: _____
   _____

10. The counseling we provide... _____
    Comments: _____
    _____

11. The referrals we give employees.. _____
    Comments: _____
    _____

12. Management consultation.. _____
    Comments: _____
    _____

13. The confidentiality of our counseling services.................................... _____
    Comments: _____
    _____

14. Our telephone/crisis counseling (HELP Line)....................................... _____
    Comments: _____
    _____

15. The accessibility of our staff... _____
    Comments: _____
    _____

Appendix

16. Our office locations... _____
    Comments: _____
    _____

17. Special workshops/training.. _____
    Comments: _____
    _____

18. Statistical reports (SCORE).. ___ ___
    Comments: _____
    _____

19. Other: _____ _____
    Comments: _____
    _____

20. Are there any services we need to improve? _____
    _____
    _____
    _____
    _____

21. Are there any services we do not have, but should? _____
    _____
    _____
    _____
    _____

22. Finally we would like your name and any other comments, if you wish.
    My name: _____
    Company: _____
    Comments: _____
    _____
    _____
    _____
    _____

Please use the back for any additional comments. When finished, return the questionnaire in the enclosed envelope. No postage is required.

Thank you

Jerry Spicer, Director
Employee Assistance Services

The EAP Solution

Figure 24

EMPLOYEE ASSISTANCE
A HAZELDEN SERVICE

Utilization Report

Contract: Sample—Quarterly Report
Reporting Period: 08/01/84 to 10/31/84   Contract Date: 02/01/84

	This Report	Contract Yr. To Date		This Report	Contract Yr. To Date
Number of Clients:			**Referral Source:**		
EAS-Office	3	10	Supervisor (Formal)	1	9
HELP LINE	73	191	Supervisor (Informal)	7	17
Lawrence & Associates	4	14	Family	7	16
Shore & Associates	4	9	Other Employee	1	3
Psych Health Mngment.	6	12	HELP LINE	26	40
Occupational Serv. Ct.	7	20	Self	61	179
Family Serv.	2	5	Other	5	14
West Cntrl. Comm. Serv.	0	1	**Reason for Contact:**		
Other	9	16	Program Information	4	10
Client Background:			Problem Assessment	98	240
Employee	91	238	Mgmt. Consultation	3	18
Family Member	17	38	Re-Assessment	1	3
Don't Know	0	2	Other	2	7
Male	73	194	**Assessed Problem:**	**Most Significant**	
Female	34	83	Educational	0	0
Average Age	36	37	Occupational	3	10
Employee Department:			Job-Stress	10	21
Marketing Division	58	125	Emotional	10	33
Production	1	13	Financial	5	14
Personnel	0	2	Legal	15	26
Finance	17	33	Client Alc/Drug Use	4	14
Transportation	1	4	Physical Health	3	5
Administration	1	5	Family Alc/Drug Use	7	23
Other	8	13	Marital/Personal Rel.	29	63
Don't Know	6	18	Other Family Rel.	15	33
Employee Occupation:			Phys/Sexual Abuse	4	6
Administrative/Mgmt.	12	30	Mgmt. Consultation	1	18
Professional	6	9	Other	2	12
Technician	55	108	**Referral Made:**		
Sales	0	0	Inpatient/Hospital	1	4
Skilled Craft	7	10	Outpatient Counseling	13	36
Clerical	6	9	Individual Therapy	15	30
Operative/Maint.	1	1	Family Therapy	9	19
Labor/Unskilled	0	0	Group Therapy	0	0
Other	7	44	Self-Help Group	1	9
Don't Know	0	3	Legal Counseling	11	18
Employee Job Class:			Financial Counseling	3	7
Supervisor	17	44	Further EAP Assess	42	114
Non-Supervisor	67	104	Other	8	20
Don't Know	10	66	None	15	47
Years of Service	11	11	#Eligible Employees	6000	6000
			#Clients	108	278
			#Families	94	214
			Annualized Utilization Rate (#Families/#Eligible Employees)	6%	5%

(Individual Company Data)

1400 Park Avenue South • Minneapolis, Minnesota 55404 • (612) 349-9464 • (800) 257-7800

Appendix

Figure 25

EMPLOYEE ASSISTANCE
A HAZELDEN SERVICE

Sample Policy Statement

The objective of the Employee Assistance Program is to reduce problems in the work force and to retain valued employees. We recognize that problems of a personal nature can have an adverse effect on an employee's job performance. It is also recognized that most personal problems can be dealt with successfully when identified early and referred to appropriate care. The Employee Assistance Program provides these services through special arrangements with an outside counseling resource. The program deals with the broad range of human problems such as emotional/behavioral, family and marital, alcohol and/or drug, financial, legal, and other personal problems.

The program provides problem assessment, short term counseling and referral. Costs for these services are covered by the employer. Costs incurred for other services not covered by insurance or other benefits are the responsibility of the employee.

The policy for use of this program:

1. Management is concerned with an employee's personal problems and how they affect him/her as a person as well as how the employee's well-being influences his/her work performance.

2. The policy applies to all employees of the company no matter what their job title or responsibilities.

3. The program is available to employees or their families on a self-referral basis since problems at home can affect the job. If employees or family members have personal problems that may benefit from assistance, they are encouraged to use the program.

4. Participation in the program will not jeopardize an employee's job security, promotional opportunities or reputation.

5. All records and discussions of personal problems will be handled in a confidential manner. These records will be kept by the designated counseling resource and will not become a part of the employee's personnel file.

6. Employees will be encouraged to seek assistance to determine if personal problems are causing unsatisfactory job performance. If performance problems are corrected, no further action will be taken. If performance problems persist, the employee will be subject to normal corrective procedures.

7. All levels of management are responsible for using this program when appropriate to assist in resolving job performance problems related to personal problems.

8. Sick leave may be granted for treatment or rehabilitation on the same basis as for other health problems. Consideration will also be given for the use of annual leave or leave without pay if sick leave is not available.

9. This policy does not alter or replace existing administrative policy or contractual agreements, but serves to assist in their utilization.

1400 Park Avenue South • Minneapolis, Minnesota 55404 • (612) 349-9464 • (800) 257-7800

Other EAP materials that will interest you...

Everybody Wins
Produced by Hazelden Educational Materials
Everybody Wins uses a compelling lecture format written and narrated by Paula J. King, M.S., to deliver a complete overview of the employee assistance program. All the information a supervisor needs to understand and use EAP services is condensed into a single production. Separate guides for instructors and participants make this package ready-to-use the moment it arrives at your office. (Color, 35 minutes)

Order No. 9194H..16mm
Order No. 0578J.......................................16mm rental
Order No. 9195H..3/4" video
Order No. 0579J..3/4" rental
Order No. 9192H...1/2" VHS
Order No. 9196........................... Instruction Guide
Order No. 9197B......................... Participation Guide

Your Move
Produced by Hazelden Educational Materials
A fast-moving, close-up dramatization of a supervisor facing an employee job performance problem. Designed to train and motivate supervisors in using the EAP, it shows the real struggles, discomforts and pitfalls that a supervisor encounters when confronting a troubled employee. *Your Move* demonstrates what the EAP is and how to use it effectively when human problems begin to take a toll on an employee's productivity. (Color, 30 minutes)

Order No. 9199H..16mm
Order No. 0599J.......................................16mm rental
Order No. 9198H..3/4" video
Order No. 0598J..3/4" rental
Order No. 9203H...1/2" VHS
Order No. 9201............................. Discussion Guide

For price and order information, please call one of our Customer Service Representatives.

Hazelden
Educational Materials
Pleasant Valley Road
Box 176
Center City, MN 55012-0176

(800) 328-9000
(Toll Free. U.S. Only)
(800) 257-0070
(Toll Free. MN Only)
(800) 328-0500
(Toll Free. Film and Video Orders. U.S. Only)
(612) 257-4010
(Alaska and Outside U.S.)